Second Life,
Second Chance!

A̲ttitude

A̲spire

A̲chieve

Namaste,

Anthony A

Second Life, Second Chance!

A Teacher's Chronicle of Despair, Recovery and Triumph

Anthony Aquan-Assee
E-mail: sept231997@yahoo.com
www.anthonyaquan-assee.com

National Library of Canada Cataloguing in Publication

Aquan-Assee, Anthony
Second life, second chance! : a teacher's chronicle of despair, recovery and triumph / Anthony Aquan-Assee.

Includes bibliographical references.
ISBN 0-9732782-0-X

1. Aquan-Assee, Anthony–Health. 2. Brain damage–Patients–Canada–Biography.
3. Motorcycling injuries–Patients–Canada–Biography. I. Title.

RC387.5.A68 2003   362.1'97481'0092   C2003-902656-6

Book management:	Intuitive Design International Ltd., Peterborough, Ontario
Cover / book design:	Karen Petherick, Intuitive Design International Ltd.
Cover art:	Photodisc 2003
Photos:	Richard Pierre

Printed and bound in Canada.

DEDICATION

I would like to dedicate this book to my mother
who taught me about love and how to love.
It is through her love that a spiritual
awakening was born in me.

PROLOGUE

I sat at the St. Michael's Hospital Trauma Awareness News Conference waiting to tell the people of Toronto the story of my motorcycle accident. Looking back on my life since the accident, I can see how the pieces were interconnected. I now believe that everything in our universe is interconnected and that there are no accidents. In our journey up the ladder of life, there are only obstacles to meet and decisions to make, and these can help us grow.

We all experience short circuits in our lives. Things inevitably go wrong, making it necessary for us to regain control of ourselves, find a positive direction in our lives, and adapt to the changed social environment. This is what I, as a brain-injured person, have had to do. The difficulties I surmounted gave me the strength to handle whatever the future has in store for me.

---

*Accidents, try to change them —
it's impossible. The accident reveals man.*
~ Pablo Picasso 1881–1973

I was involved in an extremely serious motorcycle accident and sustained life-threatening internal injuries and a traumatic brain injury. I was in a coma for two weeks. I also underwent a number of surgeries because of the extensive internal injuries. The message I wanted to deliver was that hope can carry us through despair.

Second Life, Second Chance!

Can there be a return to life after these kinds of injuries? My family and the doctors at St. Michael's Hospital would ask that question in the days and months following the accident. Neurosurgery, open heart surgery, lung surgery, general surgery, orthopedic surgery and plastic surgery would keep the Aquan-Assee family embracing hope in order to hold back the fear of death. The aftershocks of injury would radiate far, and be felt by many.

But I survived to tell my story. I was the third speaker at this news conference so I had to wait and listen to the others. I pondered where my future would lead me. What paths will I travel and what other challenges will I face? I was once told that the best predictor of the future is the past. The past lays the groundwork for the present, which in turn lays the groundwork for the future. Where would my past lead me, I wondered.

Then it was time for me to tell the story of my struggle, a story filled with pain, sadness and tears, achievement and euphoria, and a voracious appetite for growth. I have discovered many solutions to my daily problems since that fateful day, September 23, 1997, when I saw the light. It was as if I were hovering above it all, watching my motorcycle collide with the car, seeing my battered body lying on the ground, some distance from the point of the collision. A new journey was beginning, a second life and a second chance, where I would find myself challenging many of my previously held beliefs.

Nearly dying forced me to embark on a journey of self-discovery and spiritual growth that involved finding a way out of the daily torment of brain damage. The accident left me in pieces, physically, cognitively, emotionally and spiritually. Sadness, fear, despair, anger and pain throbbed through me every minute.

A brain injury, which is what I live with daily, is an invisible disability, one that the rest of society cannot see. A brain injury causes drastic emotional, intellectual and physical changes within a person. It has caused me massive pain and taken me on a journey down a very lonely path.

A man paints with his brains and not with his hands.
~ Michelangelo 1474 — 1564

But, I have seen the light at the end of the tunnel, and I now continue to walk towards that light. I want to share with you my painful journey as a brain-injured person.

This book is divided into two different sections. I tell my story in part one. In part two, I discuss the lessons I have learned and the tools that have helped me continue my climb up the ladder of my life.

It has been difficult to tell my story while living with the effects of a traumatic brain injury. I don't remember much from the early stages of my recovery. I have relied on my mother and other family members to help tell my story during those times. In addition, interviews with the many professionals that have worked with me, including those at St. Michael's Hospital and Credit Valley Hospital, videos and journal entries have also helped me put together the pieces of my life so that I could tell this story.

This book has been written in the first person wherever it is possible. Everything that happened while I hovered between life and death has been written in the third person. By telling my story, I hope to educate, motivate and encourage others to find the strength within themselves to climb the ladder of their own lives. In the words of St. Francis of Assisi, "Where there is despair, there is hope."

Courage is like love;
it must have hope to nourish it.
~ Napoleon Bonaparte 1769–1821

My recovery and rehabilitation would not have been possible without the love of my family. Their strength and dedication have helped to bring pardon to injury. Because of their love I have learned that through giving we also receive.

My recovery was also achieved with the help and commitment of many people who work behind the scenes, and whose assistance I may not have acknowledged, but my gratitude remains unending to all who have come into my life and touched my heart in their own particular way.

Thank you for allowing me to share my story with you.

God Bless you,
Anthony Aquan-Assee

Everywhere in life, the true question is not what
we gain, but what we do.
~ Thomas Carlyle 1795–1881

Anthony and his mother, Josephine Aquan-Assee.

Second Life, Second Chance!

A Teacher's Chronicle of Despair, Recovery and Triumph

THE EGG SANDWICH

I woke up excited on the morning of September 23, 1997, because there was a touch football practice that morning. I was a special education teacher at Fern Avenue Public School in Toronto and I also coached the senior boys' touch football team. I had spent the night at my girlfriend Sherry's house, as I often did. I was thinking about the football practice as I got myself ready to go to school that morning. I didn't want to be late, so when Sherry asked me if I wanted an egg sandwich for breakfast, I said, "Thanks, but I don't have time. I have a practice this morning." She made great egg sandwiches, but I was more interested in getting to my football practice. "I really have to get going." Sherry made the egg sandwich anyway but I refused to eat it despite her persistent offers. It smelled so good, but I didn't want to disappoint the boys on the team. I left the egg sandwich uneaten on the plate. It was a decision that would change the course of my life forever.

The roads we take are more important than the goals we announce. Decisions determine destiny.

~ Frederick Speakman

THE STREETSVILLE GO STATION

I flooded the engine trying to start my motorcycle, making it even more difficult to get it started. In retrospect, if I had given up trying to start my bike, I would have avoided the accident. I persisted, however, because it's not in my nature to give up. I pulled out of the driveway around 7:25 a.m., still thinking about the football practice. I wondered what plays we should focus on to prepare us for our next game, which would hopefully take us to the playoffs. During the previous week, our quarterback had not been feeling well and I wondered if he would be able to play.

As I turned left onto Thomas Road and started to go up the slight incline, the traffic slowed down. Traffic was heavy but began to move faster as I started through the intersection directly in front of the Streetsville GO Station in Mississauga. It was there that a car making an unsafe left-hand turn smashed into me. The driver apparently had not seen me crossing the intersection. As a result, my motorcycle was destroyed and I was sent soaring into the next phase of my life.

THE LIGHT

I was floating upwards, seeing the accident take place as if I were a spirit in the sky looking down a tunnel filled with a very bright light. I felt a wonderful sense of peace. Even though I was witnessing an accident that was going to change the course of my life, I felt very calm, as if I were merely an observer. Where am I? What am I seeing? I wondered. It felt so peaceful up there. I saw my motorcycle tilting to the right and veering sharply to avoid the car that was coming straight at it. Swerving quickly to avoid the car was the wrong maneuver because the car was travelling too fast. The bike was tilted far to the right, my right leg touching the ground. Unable to avoid the oncoming car, I couldn't avoid the collision.

The accident would give me the opportunity to become a new person who could learn from his past mistakes and work to rectify them. But it would require a tremendous effort to climb the individual steps up the ladder of this new life. In order to continue to climb, I could never give up.

Never, never, never, never give up.
~ Winston Churchill

THE PARAMEDICS AND THE GLASGOW COMA SCALE

The paramedics arrived at the scene to find me crumpled on the street some distance from my motorcycle, the helmet still on my head. I was bleeding from my mouth and ears and had no vital signs. They struggled to find a pulse. Nothing! There was no response to any type of sensory stimulation. It seemed futile. The paramedics' assessment, based on the Glasgow Coma Scale, gave me the lowest score: three. This assessment shows neurological responsiveness, and it indicated that I was brain-dead. A normal person with all their senses intact would score 15. The doctors later told me I was so unresponsive I achieved the same score as a table or chair.

They rushed me to the emergency room at Credit Valley Hospital in Mississauga. But they couldn't deal with the extent of my injuries so I was airlifted to St. Michael's Hospital Trauma Unit in Toronto. According to the paramedics, there didn't appear to be much hope. I had been deprived of oxygen for some time. I also appeared to have many internal injuries in addition to a serious head injury.

THE PHONE CALL

That morning, Josephine Aquan-Assee received the phone call every mother dreads. A grade 2 teacher, she was called out of her classroom to take a call from a police officer. "I'm sorry to inform you that your son, Anthony, has been involved in a very serious motorcycle accident," the officer told Josephine. Josephine's thoughts immediately flashed to the scene of an accident on Thomas Road she had noticed out of the corner of her eye while driving to school that morning. Her school was close to where Anthony's girlfriend lived but she hadn't known who was involved in the accident.

The traffic had been redirected and it appeared to be a serious accident. At the time, Josephine prayed silently to herself that no one was badly injured. Now, before the police officer mentioned any further details, she knew the accident she had seen on her way to school had involved her son. Josephine needed to know just how serious the accident was. With a feeling of dread she asked softly, "Is he going to be okay?" The police officer told her he thought she should get down to St. Michael's Hospital immediately. Josephine was distraught. She tried to get a hold of Anthony's father, Kenneth, but was unsuccessful. She was not in any shape to drive, so another teacher drove her home.

Anxious and worried, she went into the house and ran straight downstairs to the computer room. Her mouth was dry and she couldn't speak but she had to tell Kenneth the terrible news. Seeing him at the computer, she said urgently, "Kenneth hurry up and get off of the computer. Anthony's been in an accident. We have to get to St. Michael's Hospital. Why couldn't I reach you? The phone was busy all the time! We've got to go now. Hurry up!"

Kenneth just sat there with a dazed look on his face, unable to process what his frantic wife was telling him. "What?" was all he could muster, looking at her incredulously.

"Anthony's been in an accident. We need to go to St. Michael's Hospital now!" Josephine repeated with an escalating sense of urgency.

Shutting down the computer, Kenneth dashed upstairs yelling, "Let's get going."

THE JOURNEY TO ST. MICHAEL'S HOSPITAL

They were both quiet during the drive to the hospital, thinking about all the "what ifs" of the situation. They wondered what was happening to their son and where he was in the hospital.

Josephine had a feeling of dread all the way in the car. She prayed that Anthony was safe and in good hands. Kenneth concentrated on the drive and did not speak, but his mind was racing with a million thoughts.

When they got to St. Michael's, Josephine saw an ambulance at the emergency entrance and her heart sank even lower. As she walked by the ambulance, she was weak from anxiety and struggled to walk up the steps and through the emergency doors. Josephine and Kenneth approached the reception desk and noticed a lot of people standing around. Kenneth stood behind his wife as she spoke to a female attendant in what appeared to be the reception booth. "My son has been involved in an accident and he was brought here," she said, expecting them to know who her son was. Her anxiety was almost unbearable and she struggled to control her quavering voice.

The attendant did not respond immediately and then after what seemed like an eternity, she asked, "Who is your son?"

"His name is Anthony Aquan-Assee," whispered Josephine. The fear of the unknown tightened her throat, brought a throbbing pain to her head, and caused her eyes to well up with tears.

The attendant, apparently oblivious to the turmoil inside Josephine, said, "Please go with the nurse and sit in the waiting room. Someone will come to speak to you about your son as more information becomes available."

Afraid to ask, Josephine whispered, "Is he dead?"

Seeing the fear in her eyes, the attendant replied quietly, "No, but you will have to go and wait for more information."

Until the day of his death,
no man can be sure of his courage.
~ Jean Anouilh, 1920–1987

THE WAIT

Kenneth and Josephine, feeling discouraged, went with the nurse around the corner to the waiting room. Josephine anxiously scanned the gurneys in the hallway to see if Anthony was lying on one of them. But she didn't see her son, nor did she see or hear any clues that indicated he was nearby, although she knew he must be. She desperately wanted to help her son, but knew his fate was in the hands of the medical professionals at St. Michael's. The waiting room was very untidy with coffee cups and water bottles lying everywhere. But the room and the voices of the other people ceased to exist as Anthony's parents struggled with the need to know what was happening to their son.

Some time passed before a doctor came to tell them Anthony was in surgery and they would have to wait to find out anything more about his condition. This doctor could not say what the outcome of the surgery would be, but his manner was reassuring and calming.

Anthony's surgery was to stop the internal bleeding. His spleen had been ruptured and the doctors needed to remove it. They also needed to stitch up his lacerated intestines and liver to stop the loss of blood.

Following the surgery, Anthony was taken for a CAT scan

of his head. The doctors discovered there was bleeding in his brain, increasing the pressure on the brain and possibly causing further brain damage. It was imperative that neurosurgery be performed to insert a ventricular catheter into Anthony's head. This catheter would monitor the intracranial pressure (ICP) and would also drain the excess fluids from his brain.

These initial surgeries were critical for Anthony's survival, but the doctor felt his parents didn't need to know that yet.

As Josephine and Kenneth later recounted, they were in a state of shock and feared the worst for Anthony. Josephine sat restlessly in a chair wanting to do something, but knowing there was nothing she could do. Time ceased to matter as they sat in the waiting room in a daze. Josephine kept wondering what was happening to Anthony. The long wait, the hushed nature of the doctors, and the fact that this was the main trauma hospital in downtown Toronto, led her to believe that Anthony was in very serious condition.

After an endless eight-hour wait, a doctor came out and told them Anthony was being taken to the ninth floor neuro-trauma intensive care unit. They would be re-evaluating his condition shortly.

Kenneth and Josephine went up to the ninth floor feeling like robots, devoid of emotion. As they exited the elevator, they saw a room filled with people, as well as people sitting in the blue chairs that lined the hallway. There was no room for privacy. In the waiting room, a young couple sat beside an older woman. Their faces were somber and the silence was interrupted by the fitful coughing of a man sitting in the hallway. Kenneth guessed that these people were all visitors. On the wall outside the waiting room was a buzzer that allowed them to contact the I.C.U. Josephine gestured to Kenneth and then, determined to see her son, extended her finger towards the buzzer. She stopped when she heard a cheerful voice saying, "Hello, can I help you find someone?"

A man wearing a green jacket sat at a desk with a sign on it that said, Volunteer on Duty. "We're trying to find our son, Anthony. A doctor told us downstairs that he was being brought to the neuro-trauma intensive care unit. Are we in the right place?"

The young man pulled out a sheet of paper with names on it and examined in carefully. "What's his last name?" he asked.

"Aquan-Assee," Josephine replied.

"Ah, yes, here he is. He's in bed number 10. First, let me check with the nurse to see if it's okay for you to go inside and see him."

He left Josephine and Kenneth standing there, exasperated that they had to wait again before they could see Anthony. After several minutes of restless waiting, while the hallway filled with people and then emptied again, the volunteer returned.

With an impassive look on his face, he escorted Kenneth and Josephine to bed number 10 in the I.C.U., where Anthony lay unconscious.

THE HORROR IN THE I.C.U.

Seeing their son, they couldn't believe their eyes. Anthony was the size of the bed. His body was swollen, battered and bloody. He looked like a giant blow-up doll. His head was larger than a basketball, his face was black and blue and his eye sockets had disappeared. There were thick staples in his temples holding together a massive incision on his skull. His face was so swollen Josephine was afraid the bones were crushed.

She looked at her barely recognizable son but there were no words to describe what she saw. It was terrible.

Josephine turned away from the sight of her once handsome son. Tears welled up in her eyes and Kenneth reached out his arm to support her. Kenneth breathed a deep sigh and looked up to the ceiling as if he were asking God, "Why?"

Many strange pieces of equipment stood around the bed. Anthony had a tube in his mouth that led to a machine beside his bed and there were cables with some pads at the ends of them stuck to his chest. These cables extended to what looked like a computer monitor with several waves oscillating on it.

The nurse at Anthony's bedside introduced herself. She explained what they had done with Anthony in the surgery and why he looked so swollen. Kenneth asked the nurse what the equipment was used for. She told him that the tube in Anthony's mouth was attached to a ventilator that was used to pump oxygen into his lungs. "The round pads on his chest are called ECG leads, and these are electrodes that measure the electrical currents generated by his heart. This computer monitor that the cables are attached to enables us to monitor his vital signs, such as his blood pressure and his pulse."

Kenneth and Josephine stood by Anthony's bedside in a state of complete shock. Nothing could have prepared them for what they saw. With the fear of death in her eyes, Josephine reached out to hold her son's hand, hoping he would open his eyes and look at her. Seeing the look of desperation on Josephine's face, the nurse quietly told his parents that Anthony was in a deep coma and would not be able to respond to them.

Anthony's parents left the I.C.U. and went into the hallway to regain their composure. How could anyone survive what their son had gone through?

A young doctor finally appeared and approached Kenneth and Josephine slowly, his white coat tightly buttoned up as if to guard against the sadness so prevalent in the I.C.U. He introduced himself to Anthony's parents as one of the doctors on duty in the neuro-trauma I.C.U.

He said, "Your son has been in a horrific accident and is in extremely serious condition. I would suggest that you prepare for the worst." After a pause he gently suggested, "Don't expect too much. I want you to think about the quality of life Anthony would have wanted. We don't know if he'll live through the night, but you should go home and have some rest, because you'll need all of your strength in the next few days."

ANTHONY'S SISTER

That night Josephine called Anthony's sister Jasmin in Boston to break the news. She told her about Anthony's grim prognosis. "The doctors have not given him much chance of survival. You need to come home right away."

Jasmin arrived at the hospital the next morning and met Josephine in the I.C.U. waiting room. Her face was streaked with tears and her eyes were red from continuous crying. She reached out to hug her mother and said between sobs, "Mother, I'm so sorry this has happened. I'll do anything I can." Jasmin, a clinical psychologist in Boston, was accustomed to supporting other people during times of crisis. Now, she was faced with a crisis that would rock the very foundation of her own family. For them, the challenge would be to maintain hope.

Jasmin and Josephine went into the I.C.U. and saw a large black box beside Anthony with wires attached to his head. Josephine was apprehensive. "This computer wasn't here yesterday, Jasmin. I wonder what it is? I don't see any of the other patients with this piece of equipment." A doctor later told them the black box monitored brain activity, giving a clearer picture of the neurological activity in Anthony's brain.

Josephine and Jasmin sat on either side of Anthony's bed, moving occasionally to get out of the way of the nurses who were constantly monitoring the machines and gadgets attached to him. The nurses also made sure that all the tubes were positioned correctly. They recorded the data from their examinations in Anthony's case-history book.

Josephine sat quietly at the bedside feeling bewildered, shocked, anxious and numb, yet compelled to keep up a mask of calm and equanimity. Jasmin was more interactive and would frequently look at the notes the nurses had written. She wanted to ensure that her brother was receiving the best care possible. She had worked as part of a team in a number of hospitals and was interested in the medical side of Anthony's care. The nurses often asked Josephine and Jasmin to leave the I.C.U. so they could complete various procedures with Anthony. Then the two women would sit with the other visitors in the waiting room until they were allowed to return and sit by Anthony's bed.

This routine continued the entire day until Anthony's two brothers, Jonathan and Michael, arrived with their father in the evening. Sherry came later in the evening when she could get a babysitter for her children.

The entire family, along with Sherry, was then allowed into the I.C.U. to be with Anthony. Standing at his bedside, they spoke to Anthony even though he didn't respond. They believed he could hear them although he showed no signs of awareness. They told him how loved he was, how important he was to the family, and how much they wanted him to communicate with them. They wanted him to know they supported him in his struggle for survival and would always be there for him.

They hoped he would respond positively to their words of encouragement. They let Anthony know who was there at his bedside, and they asked him to let them know if he could hear them. They also told him they were bringing some family pictures the next day, so that when he awoke he would see familiar faces that might trigger his memory.

The next shift of nurses came on and the family wanted to remain at Anthony's bedside, but they were asked to leave while the next shift of nurses was brought up-to-date on the patients. At this point, Josephine realized how tired they all were and decided it would be best to go home. Everyone needed a good rest to prepare for the next day.

Sherry decided to stay overnight at the hospital and go home when Josephine returned the next morning. This became an important part of Anthony's recovery. Someone was always there to look after his needs, to communicate with him and stimulate his mind. It was the family's strategy to help restore Anthony to consciousness. They are convinced it played an important part in his recovery.

The next morning Josephine, Jasmin and Jonathan sat at the kitchen table looking at each other, feeling fearful and uncertain. They were thinking of ways to help Anthony when Jasmin had an idea. "Do you have any of Anthony's favourite music tapes?" she asked Jonathan.

"No," he said, "but I know what music he likes. Why?"

"Well, I've heard that people in a coma can still hear things, they just can't respond. Maybe if we play some of

Anthony's favourite music, he'll hear it and recognize it and it might stimulate his brain."

"That's a great idea," agreed Josephine. "Jonathan, see if you can find some of Anthony's music tapes." Jonathan found the tapes within five minutes and put one of them into his own Walkman. He gave the Walkman to his mother but told her he didn't want to go with her to the hospital. Josephine saw that he had been crying. She knew Jonathan looked up to his older brother and couldn't bear to see him in such a helpless state.

It was Saturday and Josephine knew that Jonathan and Michael were going to ride their bikes while she was at the hospital. With the memory of Anthony lying comatose in the I.C.U., all swollen up with cuts all over his body, she told them both to get into her car; they were going to buy bicycle helmets. Jonathan and Michael moaned and protested but she insisted. "It's unacceptable that you're riding around without helmets. I don't want anything to happen to you like what happened to your brother."

The boys stopped protesting and went with her. They bought the best bicycle helmets in the store.

MENTAL STIMULATION

Jasmin and Josephine were anxious to get back to the hospital. They were encouraged by Jasmin's idea and hoped that playing Anthony's music to him might help bring him out of the coma. In the I.C.U. they saw Sherry sitting beside the bed. Josephine noted Anthony's unusual posture. His arms were extended stiffly at his sides and turned inwards. His legs were also stiffly extended. The nurse on duty smiled at Jasmin and Josephine and told them that Anthony's body posture was not unusual for someone in a coma. What they didn't know was that this type of posture was referred to as decerebrate posturing or extensor posturing and was indicative of deterioration of the upper brain stem. The nurse didn't tell them that the prognosis was very poor for patients who exhibited this type of body posture.

After Sherry went home, Jasmin placed the earphones of Jonathan's Walkman over Anthony's ears and they both looked at him with anticipation, hoping for a sign that he could hear the music. But he just lay there oblivious to the world around him.

Josephine and Jasmin stayed with Anthony for the day and then Kenneth came with Jonathan and Michael in the evening. There had been no improvement. Anthony remained in a deep coma and didn't respond to any type of stimulation. When Kenneth arrived, Josephine quietly said to him, "Anthony is still with us. I think he'll make it even though he's not moving or showing any signs of life at the moment. Something tells me he has an inner strength that will pull him through this." She continued to cling to hope despite her despair.

The nurse asked Anthony's parents to wait outside the I.C.U. while she did the Glasgow Coma Score Assessment. The assessment was done every hour to check for neurological responses. The nurses would see if he could open his eyes, if he was able to respond verbally, and if he moved in response to a stimulus. Often, the nurse would induce pain to see if Anthony would move away from the painful stimulus. But Anthony still didn't respond to any type of stimulation.

Sherry arrived later in the evening to stay with him during the night while the family was at home. Before she left the hospital, Josephine explained to her how they had put headphones on Anthony's ears and played music for him. Sherry wasn't discouraged that Anthony hadn't responded to the music. She was determined to help him regain consciousness.

At dawn, Jasmin and Josephine returned to the hospital and met Sherry in the waiting room. As they waited to go into the I.C.U., Jasmin opened her book, turning the pages absent-mindedly. Sherry turned to her and said excitedly, "Jasmin, let's read, *The Celestine Prophecy* to Anthony; it's his favourite book."

"What a great idea!" said Jasmin. "It might help us reach him."

They took turns reading the book for days to come. It was difficult to keep reading when Anthony didn't respond at all. They hoped that if he could recognize their voices, he would realize they were there for him. With loving patience they persisted, despite the odds against ever reaching him. The nurses had never seen this level of support in the I.C.U.

Each day was a journey down a road never travelled. At first the family felt fear, anxiety, depression and despair, but they never gave up hope; they always believed there was a glint of optimism on the horizon. Josephine, Kenneth, Jasmin, Jonathan, Michael and Sherry would sit by Anthony's bedside every day and night hoping to see some sign that he was still inside this lifeless mass of battered flesh lying on the bed. They worked co-operatively, focusing totally on Anthony. The day-to-day routine of their lives was set aside so they could be there for him. They could only hope and pray that the Lord would bring pardon to his injuries.

The family knew they needed to have a plan in place so that when Anthony came out of his coma he would receive the maximum support from them. Pictures of family members were brought in and placed on the IV stand beside his bed so he would see them when he opened his eyes. They wanted him to know his family was with him in this alien environment.

THE DECISION

Anthony had been in a coma for over a week when Dr. X and the other members of the medical team spoke to Josephine, Jasmin and Sherry as part of a case consultation. They advised Josephine to think about the quality of life Anthony would want. They told her it was unlikely he would ever emerge from the coma, and even if he did, he would most likely be a vegetable for the rest of his life. Josephine realized she was now faced with deciding whether to have her son removed from life support. If Anthony was going to be a vegetable for the rest of his life, what should they do? Josephine wasn't ready to make that decision yet. She wanted to go home and discuss it with Kenneth.

On the GO Train back to Oakville, Josephine contemplated what she would say to her husband. What should they do? Would they have to deal with the death of their son? She knew she wasn't ready to accept what the medical experts were telling her.

Josephine walked into the house with tears in her eyes. Kenneth looked at her, unable to find the right words. "What happened today?" he asked. "Were there any changes with him?"

Josephine's voice quavered as she told him what the doctors had said. Kenneth was depressed by the devastating news but knew his wife needed his support. They decided they had to prove to themselves and the doctors that Anthony was still alive and "in there."

The next day Kenneth walked into the ICU determined to get a response from his son. At the bedside he saw three doctors doing their various assessments. They stepped aside so Kenneth could approach his son.

"Anthony!" he said. "Are you in there, Anthony? Move your feet! Move your toes!" Anthony's mother and Dr. X watched and said nothing. To everyone's amazement, Anthony moved his toe, and then he gripped Kenneth's hand and squeezed it. Kenneth gasped and turned to see the doctors' reaction. "He squeezed my hand!" he exclaimed.

Then Anthony moved his arm. Dr. X told Anthony to open his eyes. After a while, they could see Anthony's eyeballs moving beneath his closed eyelids; he was clearly struggling to open his eyes. Dr. X then told Anthony to move his toes. And again, Anthony responded by moving his toes.

Dr. X, a gentle and kindly person, turned to Anthony's parents and said, "It looks like we were premature in our diagnosis." Anthony's parents were ecstatic. Their son was alive.

DEBT OF GRATITUDE

All the assessments and observations the doctors had available to them indicated there was no hope. The computer equipment also showed that Anthony was unresponsive and there was little chance of his regaining consciousness. What nobody realized was that nothing is impossible. There are some things in life that don't have a "scientific" explanation. Through the doctors' expertise, their devotion to saving lives and the fantastic care that Anthony received in the I.C.U., the impossible became possible.

• • • • •

FEAR AND CONFUSION

I opened my eyes and woke up from what seemed like an eternity. I had been in a deep coma for close to two weeks. Where was I? What was I doing here? Why were all these tubes in my body? The fear and the physical pain were overwhelming. What had happened to me? Sherry was standing beside my bed and her face lit up when I opened my eyes. She was smiling and spoke to me reassuringly, telling me I had been in a motorcycle accident and was in St. Michael's Hospital. The questions racing through my mind were endless. I kept slipping in and out of the present, unable to concentrate on something for longer than a few seconds. I felt as though my brain were turning on for a brief moment and then shutting off, as if it had a short circuit. I knew my brain was not working properly and that scared me. Knowing I couldn't communicate, Sherry moved closer to me, hoping her presence would give me some security.

The pain that throbbed through my body was excruciating, and was aggravated by the many tubes in my chest draining the fluids. It felt like an elephant was sitting on my chest, splitting it apart. I wanted someone to help me, but I was unable to speak. I felt like I was trapped in hell.

• • • • •

Sherry couldn't contain her excitement. She ran out of the I.C.U. to find Josephine and Kenneth and tell them that Anthony had opened his eyes. The day she had been praying for had finally come. All she could think was, Thank You, God! Sherry always believed Anthony would never leave her and now he was back. Sherry saw Josephine and Kenneth talking to the social worker. She ran up to them and exclaimed, "Anthony just opened his eyes. Come and see. Quickly!"

Josephine stared at Sherry in astonishment. Hoping they would be in time, Kenneth and Josephine ran back into the I.C.U. When they got to his bedside, Anthony's eyes were open.

"This is great, Anthony!" Josephine said to him. "We're all here." They stayed for several minutes, until he closed his eyes and went back to sleep. Despite having opened his eyes, however, Anthony was not yet responding to any stimulation. It was as if he had lapsed into a deep coma again. Still feeling anxious and frustrated, his parents decided to go home and rest, hoping the next day would bring more good news.

Sherry stayed at the hospital that night and spent as much time as she could in the I.C.U. She tried to sleep in the waiting room but found herself lying awake, thinking of Anthony and his open eyes.

Josephine was up early the next day, anxious to get back to the hospital. She couldn't stop thinking of the moment the night before when Anthony opened his eyes. She took the 8:35 a.m. GO Train from Clarkson so she could be at the hospital in time to relieve Sherry, who needed to get back to her three children. Kenneth, Jonathan and Michael would arrive later in the evening. They had kept up this routine, making sure Anthony was never left alone. As they later learned, it had a significant effect on his recovery.

Anthony's accident brought out a co-operative team effort in the family that revealed how strong the ties between them were. While one door may have been closed, many new doors were opened. Friends and even strangers offered to help Anthony and his family. Prayers, thoughts, visits, gifts, cards, food for the family and kind words were all part of a universal energy directed towards his recovery.

Josephine was nervous as she walked into the I.C.U., fearing Anthony might have lapsed back into a coma. When she saw him, however, he was lying in bed with his eyes open, looking straight up at the ceiling. Her heart went to her throat. "Hi Anthony, this is Mom," she said. She took his hand and he squeezed hers in recognition. He turned his head and made eye contact with his mother. "Anthony, this is wonderful," she told him. "Don't worry. You're here and you're alive." He couldn't speak because of the respirator in his mouth, but his eyes showed that he understood. A nurse was standing close by and said to Josephine, "He's done more than the doctors every thought was possible." Josephine beamed at her son and waited patiently for more signs of communication. Anthony closed his eyes and drifted off to sleep.

The wait seemed endless and Josephine felt completely alone. Kenneth would not arrive until later in the evening when Jonathan and Michael finished their school day. Sitting at Anthony's bedside in silence, she thought about how difficult their schedule of visits to the hospital was. Rigorous as it was, though, they had all managed to support each other without any conflicts.

The silent waiting was occasionally interrupted by the shouted demands of the patient in the bed across from Anthony. The man was paralyzed from the neck down and immobilized by a halo vest. His head, neck and chest were locked in the rigid frame, preventing any movement. He frequently cried out for help, raging against his fate.

Time ceased to matter in the I.C.U. There were no windows to distinguish night from day. Josephine sat beside Anthony's bed and watched him and the other patients in the I.C.U. She would occasionally take coffee breaks with some of the people she and Kenneth had met in the waiting room and learned they shared a similar tragedy.

She gained comfort and support by sharing the day-to-day details with people whose suffering was like hers. Their conversations were frequently disrupted by events in the I.C.U., but they gained understanding through their common bond of pain.

Kenneth, Jonathan and Michael arrived while Josephine was talking to a woman whose son was also in the hospital. Kenneth went up to Josephine and hugged her, holding his breath and saying to himself, "Please God, let Anthony get better." Holding her husband tightly, Josephine could feel the tension in his body. She whispered to him, "Anthony's eyes were open this morning when I arrived at the hospital, but not for long. They've been closed all day."

They went looking for Jane, the head nurse, who was always very supportive of the family. Hearing the news about Anthony opening his eyes, she said, "Anthony's very lucky to have all of you." She explained that most of the people in the I.C.U. didn't have family or anybody else supporting them the way Anthony did.

CONTINUING TO QUESTION

In the long periods spent in the I.C.U. Josephine and Kenneth got to know the different nurses. Some nurses were more talkative than others. Their happy spirit was contagious and made things easier in the unhappy environment. Some nurses were more receptive to Josephine's constant questions about Anthony's prognosis and the function of the equipment that he was hooked up to. What did the different readings on the equipment indicate? Did a particular reading mean that her son was not getting enough oxygen? What was the next procedure he would undergo and what did certain body movements indicate neurologically? It helped Josephine stay up-to-date with her son's care. Sherry also asked the nurses a lot of questions.

The constant questions made some of the nurses feel uneasy but most welcomed their devotion to Anthony. The nurses continued to work hard with him and Sherry and Josephine were always there keeping tabs on him as well. The family and Sherry were like the eyes and ears of the medical team, supporting Anthony through the difficult days as new worries and concerns continued to surface. When Josephine saw a large cast on Anthony's right leg, she thought, what next? The kneecap was broken and three of the four ligaments were torn. The doctors told her these injuries would require orthopedic surgery in the future.

RECOVERING IN THE I.C.U.

In the four days since Anthony had opened his eyes, he gained enough strength to move his hands and pull out the connections to the heart monitor on his chest. They irritated him and he constantly tried to remove them. He opened his eyes intermittently and stared vacantly into space unless his attention was forcefully redirected elsewhere.

On the fifth day, his parents were sitting at the bedside wondering if Anthony knew they were there. His eyes were closed and they hoped for a sign from him. He appeared to be unaware of their presence and his own body movements. He seemed to still be in a coma. His legs moved constantly, often kicking anyone that came too close to the bedside. Diane, one of the nurses that regularly looked after Anthony, often held his hands to prevent him from pulling the heart monitors from his chest. She told Josephine he was very wild and hard to control.

That evening Anthony not only tried to pull off the heart monitors, but he also tried to pull the breathing tube from his throat and managed to pull the IV from his wrist. He was so restless, Diane tied his hands to the bed's metal frame to prevent him from pulling out any more tubes. In the days that followed, the nurses insisted that his hands remain tied unless Kenneth and Josephine promised to restrain him.

The next night, they sat at the bedside as usual and monitored the constant, erratic movements of their son. He was trying, unsuccessfully, to free himself from the multitude of wires and gadgets that were monitoring his vital signs. Josephine tried to distract him by asking him to hold up two fingers. It took several minutes for his brain to comprehend what she said, but he slowly responded by holding up two fingers. Josephine then said to him, "Do you know that you are a teacher and that you are teaching us right now?" He responded by nodding his head.

Laura, one of the nurses helping Diane, looked over in astonishment at the interaction taking place between Josephine and her son. She told her, "Anthony continues to surprise and amaze us." Josephine nodded in appreciation, proud that her son could amaze the medical community.

Anthony's wild reactions intensified when Jonathan and Michael came into the I.C.U. Tired of sitting in the waiting room, they wanted to see their brother, but as soon as they were beside him, Anthony began to pinch and strike out at them. It was as if he needed an outlet for the tension that had built up inside him after lying in bed for so long. Michael and Jonathan took the abuse, knowing their brother wasn't aware of his actions and was behaving like a wild animal. He wasn't very strong and it was easy for them to re-direct his grasping hands. Anthony soon tired and his eyes closed for the next hour.

Josephine was concerned because Anthony wasn't responding to any of the stimulation they were giving him. He didn't move when they touched him or spoke to him, despite the fact that he had recently been so uncontrollable. Josephine stroked her son's arm, worried they might have overstimulated his brain, when Anthony opened his eyes. He looked at her in bewilderment and confusion and seemed not to recognize his mother. He slipped in and out of consciousness and his look of uncertainty continued for the rest of the night and the next day.

THE TRACHEOTOMY

Sherry always made sure Anthony was as comfortable and well looked after as possible. One night she noticed his lips were swollen and cracked and appeared to be causing him pain. Worried it might be a breeding ground for bacteria, she discussed it with Jane, the head nurse. Jane agreed it was unhealthy for him to continue having a respirator in his mouth and decided they should attempt a tracheotomy. He was healthy enough to undergo another operation, so on October 8, Anthony went for tracheotomy surgery and the respirator was removed.

SPELL CHECKER COMMUNICATION

Having a tracheotomy instead of the respirator was a big relief for Anthony. He could now open his mouth. Even though he couldn't speak, he responded to questions from his mother and Sherry by scribbling words on a pad of paper. The first word he wrote after he regained consciousness was, "ALIVE!"

Anthony had trouble with his fine motor co-ordination and the words he tried to write were often illegible. On Sunday, October 12th, his younger brother Jonathan came up with the brilliant idea of bringing in his handheld spellchecker so that Anthony could type anything he wanted to communicate. When Jonathan typed "How are you?" Anthony replied by typing, "Fuckyousoldier." Laughing as she read the message, Josephine was relieved to know he could still understand and communicate using language, even though he needed practice to make his thoughts comprehensible to others.

PLASTIC SURGERY

The words Anthony typed with the spellchecker were often complex and perplexing. On the morning of October 15th, the day of his plastic surgery, he mouthed the words "I want to scream" to his mother and his face clearly showed that he was in excruciating pain. When the doctor asked him where the pain was, he responded, "In my descending wrists."

Several hours later, he was taken to the operating room for plastic surgery. At 4:45 p.m. the plastic surgeon came out and said, "Anthony's A-OK. Most of the bones in his face were broken. We placed a wire and a screw in the bone by his left eyebrow, and a plate on his broken cheek. He'll start to swell in about 48 hours." The plastic surgeon was a friendly man and Josephine and Kenneth immediately felt comfortable with him. He showed a genuine interest in them and the rest of the family. Josephine wondered how her son's handsome face would look after the plastic surgery. Was there going to be any visible scarring?

When Anthony got back to the I.C.U. Josephine was relieved to see that the incisions around the broken eye socket were almost invisible. She worried, however, when his body began to shake in spasms as if he were having an epileptic seizure. Anthony's nurse told her, "Don't worry. It's normal to shake after surgery." It didn't look normal to Josephine and she continued to worry.

For the next several days Anthony would slip in and out of consciousness. He was unable to focus his attention on anything for longer than a few seconds. The family and his friends began to realize that Anthony's recovery was going to be a long ordeal. They needed to continue with their own lives if they wanted to remain strong for him.

THE MAN WHO BROUGHT PARDON TO INJURY
SUNDAY, OCT. 19

In the middle of October, Anthony's close friend, Sam, went to a presentation at the University of Toronto by a psychologist and motivational speaker. Anthony and Sam had planned to attend this presentation by Dr. Wayne Dyer, a man they both admired and respected. They had read several of Dr. Dyer's books and tried to follow his words of wisdom. Sam sat in the auditorium thinking of how Anthony would have loved the presentation. When it was over, he went up to speak to

Dr. Dyer. The line was long. Many people wanted to speak to the man known as "The Father of Motivation." Sam wanted to tell him about Anthony. When he finally reached the front of the line, Dr. Dyer shook Sam's hand vigorously. "Hello Dr. Dyer," he said. "My name is Sam. I'm a big fan of yours. My friend Anthony is also a huge fan but he couldn't come here today because he's in a coma at St. Michael's Hospital in downtown Toronto. He was in a very serious motorcycle accident. I was wondering," Sam continued, "would you be able to go there and visit him? I know he would love it. He's read many of your books and was planning on coming here today."

Dr. Dyer's first thought was about the plane he had to catch later that day. He often received requests to help people but he didn't think he would have time to go to the hospital.

Thinking of the wonderful things he had heard about Dr. Dyer, Sam tried again with a little more urgency, "Would you please just be in his presence? Just bring your energy to his presence." Dr. Dyer thought for a moment. Sam's plea reminded him that life gives to life. "Yes," he said. I'll go." Dr. Dyer left the auditorium early so he could stop at the hospital on his way to the airport. He took the elevator to the ninth floor at St. Michael's Hospital to the Neuro-Trauma Intensive Care Unit where Anthony was lying in a coma.

A nurse greeted him as he walked in, "Hello, can I help you?"

"Ah yes, I'm here to see Anthony," said Dr. Dyer.

"Are you a doctor?" asked the nurse.

"Yes," he replied, even though he knew he wasn't the kind of doctor she meant. She pointed to where Anthony lay and he walked over to him. Dr. Dyer could see how badly damaged the young man's body was. It appeared that he might not live much longer. Dr. Dyer began to pray and meditate at the bedside, surrounding Anthony's body with a healing energy. He would later say that he brought pardon to Anthony's injured body.

As he left the hospital for the airport, Dr. Dyer thought that if Anthony could connect to the healing energy, then, one day, he would be able to walk out of the hospital. After that visit, he included Anthony in his daily prayers.

Josephine and Kenneth arrived at the hospital a short time later and Anthony's nurse, Liz, told them of the doctor's visit. She said Anthony had remained unresponsive during the entire time Dr. Dyer was there. As soon as Josephine came to Anthony's bedside, however, he opened his eyes and looked at his mother. She and Kenneth were overjoyed. They had both watched television programs featuring Dr. Dyer and always encouraged Anthony to follow his work. They never could have imagined that he would one day honour their son with his presence. Josephine thought it was a wonderful birthday present for her son, who would be turning 29 in two days.

On the morning of October 21st, preparations were underway to celebrate Anthony's birthday in the I.C.U. On this special day the doctors gave permission for him to sit up in bed with his neck supported by a neck brace. Sherry was allowed to bring in several balloons to tie to his bed. The family brought in music tapes and pictures of Anthony when he was younger. Friends also came to visit him and brought cards. Even some of the nurses joined in to sing "Happy Birthday." The confused look on Anthony's face told Josephine he didn't understand what they were celebrating. She realized there was too much sensory stimulation and too many people around the bed.

Sitting up in bed, Anthony moved continuously and struggled to remove the many wires and gadgets still connected to his body. Josephine and Kenneth held his hands to restrain him while Josephine re-directed his attention to the pen and clipboard. She asked him to write something and he wrote, "peace love prosperity and the year is 1000."

The commotion had tired Anthony and he needed a lot of sleep to recover. His mother worried when, once again, he appeared to go back into a coma and remained unresponsive for some time.

HEART SURGERY

Before Anthony's birthday, his team of doctors faced a dilemma. Should they try to prevent further brain damage or save his heart? After their initial examinations, the heart surgeons wanted to perform heart surgery immediately. They knew his aorta had been damaged and would require surgery but they didn't know the extent of the damage. The aorta is the main blood vessel that carries oxygen-rich blood away from the heart to the organs of the body. The neuro-surgeons had been concerned about the swelling in Anthony's brain ever since he arrived in the I.C.U. It was imperative that the swelling be reduced. If the open-heart surgery was performed immediately, however, the heart and lung machine and the intravenous fluids used in the surgery could aggravate the swelling in Anthony's brain and cause additional damage.

They finally decided to put off the open-heart surgery until the swelling in Anthony's brain decreased. The open-heart surgery was performed on October 24th. The surgeons discovered that the aortic arch had been severely ruptured and was only being held together by a thin piece of skin. After the blood is pumped out of the heart, it enters the aortic arch before going to the rest of the body. Any movement could have caused the skin to tear, leading to a quick death.

After the surgery, the heart surgeon assured Josephine it went well. He had placed a Dacron graft on the aorta to hold it together. He told her that if he had known just how ruptured the aortic arch was, he would never have allowed Anthony to sit up on his birthday. Another doctor told her, "It's a miracle the aorta didn't rupture completely."

LUNG SURGERY

After the heart surgery, more problems kept Anthony's family grasping for signs of hope. Josephine wept silently when they were told that a broncoscopy of his left lung revealed that it was completely blocked. His lung had been badly damaged and might have to be removed completely.

Josephine and Kenneth waited with nervous apprehension in the waiting room, trying to shut out the commotion around them and avoid the eyes of other visitors. An old man came up to them and asked, "How can I speak to a doctor in the I.C.U.?" Josephine's thoughts were on her son but Kenneth pointed to the volunteer's desk. Just then a voice came over the intercom asking the Aquan-Assee family to come into the I.C.U. Josephine looked at her husband with fear in her eyes. "What is it now?" she whispered.

In the I.C.U. they saw Anthony's heart surgeon. He told them that a thoracic surgeon at St. Joseph's hospital was going to perform Anthony's lung surgery. The extent of the injury required the expertise of this surgeon if they were to save the lung. Josephine told the doctor, "I don't want Anthony moved to St. Joseph's hospital. It will be too much for him." The doctor reassured her, "I held your son's heart in my hands. I would never do anything to harm him."

On November 6, 1997, the thoracic surgeon from St. Joseph's hospital performed the lung surgery at St. Michael's Hospital with the heart surgeon assisting him. Following the surgery, both doctors came out of the operating room to speak with Josephine and Kenneth. "We were able to save his lung, and the ruptured bronchus has been repaired." Anthony had torn the left main-stem bronchus, which is the tube that brings air to the left lung. Josephine and Kenneth hugged each other and rejoiced after hearing this. "Thank God, for this Hospital," Josephine wept.

The family kept a vigil at Anthony's bedside and at home, praying that he would recover from his injuries. Their main concern after the lung surgery was that he regain his strength. His muscles had atrophied significantly from lying in bed. He had been on a ventilator for so long his lungs were congested with fluid.

The physiotherapist, Nikki, made sure that all the secretions in the lungs were cleared out on a regular basis. She also made sure his joints didn't get too stiff by regularly exercising them. As Anthony became less dependent on the ventilator, Nikki helped him sit up in bed, often with the assistance of Josephine or Kenneth because Anthony couldn't follow Nikki's instructions. Josephine or Kenneth would also help her move him into the correct position so he could sit in a wheelchair.

One week after the lung surgery, Nikki came into the I.C.U. for her regular session with Anthony. Josephine was sitting at the bedside. "Hello Josephine," said Nikki. "How are you doing? You look very tired. How's Anthony?" Josephine smiled and looked at Anthony who was asleep. "Let's take him for a ride out of the I.C.U. today," said Nikki. "I'm going to need your help to get him into the chair. Okay?"

"Should I try to wake him up now?" Josephine asked.

"Yes, please do." Nikki replied.

Josephine worried aloud that Anthony wouldn't be able to handle sitting in the chair for a long period of time, but she knew he needed to practice every day to get stronger so he could start rehab.

• • • • •

After I was in the Intensive Care Unit for nearly two months, my family took me for a small trip to the waiting room outside of the I.C.U. I was sitting in a wheelchair and they showed me what was happening outside the Hospital. My mother pointed out the window and said, "Look, Anthony, that's the Eaton Centre. Do you remember the Eaton Centre? You used to love going there when you were younger." I thought about it but the place didn't sound familiar to me. I shook my head. I couldn't remember it. I looked out the window and saw the big buildings and the movement of the traffic. I felt afraid and anxious. I turned to my mother for comfort as if I were a small child faced with a new situation. My family eventually took me back to the I.C.U. I was exhausted, scared and uncertain. I didn't know what the future had in store for me. Once back in my bed I fell asleep immediately.

THE PENTHOUSE SUITE

I was in the Intensive Care Unit for two months before being moved to a private room on the same floor. I still didn't understand what was happening to me. Why was I living my life in this strange place? My body was in so much pain and my mind was not working. It was very difficult to turn in bed or adjust the position of my body because of the big cast on my leg. I was always in a lot of pain.

When my mother and father wheeled me into my new room, I saw the single bed in the middle of the room. There were no other beds. Sleep by myself? I thought. Where were the other people going to sleep? My mother saw the confusion on my face and said, "Anthony, this will be your own room now. You are out of the Intensive Care Unit. Isn't this better? Look, you have your own bathroom too!" (which my physical condition did not permit me to use). "This is one of the biggest private rooms here at St. Michael's. It's kind of like the hospital's penthouse suite."

I didn't understand her and thought to myself, "What's a penthouse suite?" Feeling tired, I didn't wait for an answer. I pointed to the bed and my father picked me up and carried me to it.

"Anthony, you've lost a lot of weight. You're so light," he said. He was remembering my size when I competed in judo and bodybuilding. The muscular build that I used to have, and which probably helped to save my life, was gone. Once a bodybuilding champion with a well-developed muscular frame of 190 pounds, I had shrunk to a mere 113 pounds, a direct result of the liquid diet I was fed through a naso-gastric tube that went into my nose and down to my stomach.

I also had aspirations of competing in the 2000 Olympics in Sydney, Australia, representing Canada in the sport of judo. Before my accident I was training for the national championships in order to qualify for the Olympic team. Now, I was competing against life itself and the struggle to return to my former self was the challenge.

As my father placed me on this new bed, the familiar stabbing pain in my chest, my arm and my knee returned. My entire body was bruised and was a shade of purple. The dark bruising on my left arm was especially pronounced where the bone had pierced the skin of my elbow. God, please help me! I pleaded and burst into tears of self-pity. Please, I can't take this any more. The tears rolled down my face but no one answered my prayers. How can there be a God, I thought? Why did he let this happen to me?

So began the constant pleading and questioning of myself, God, and humanity. I could not explain why I was faced with so many challenges. My life had been going so well before the accident. As I thought about these things, lying in the hospital, it became apparent to me that there were certain things in life that were beyond explanation.

Seeing my obvious discomfort, my father asked me, "Anthony, what's wrong?"

"Dad, get me a nurse."

"Why do you want a nurse?" he asked.

"I need something for the pain. My chest is killing me and so is the rest of my body."

There was a buzzer to call the nurse whenever one was needed. Determined to help me, my father pressed it and contacted the nursing station for help. The nurse came in and asked me in a softly accented voice, "Hello Anthony. Where are you in pain?"

Taking charge, my father responded, "His chest is hurting and so is his leg. He needs something for the pain." It was customary for my father to take charge in matters where his children were concerned. It made me feel like a teenager again.

The nurse had a small container with an assortment of items in it. She pulled out a needle and injected my upper arm. The painkiller made me tired and I fell asleep. When I opened my eyes the next morning, my parents were not there. They must have gone home while I slept. I spent the following days sleeping, waking only momentarily when someone came into the room.

Several days had passed when I awoke one morning to see my mother, father, Michael and Jonathan standing by the door. Jonathan was smiling and pointing a video camera straight at me. "Anthony, I want to film you so that you can see yourself when you get out of here."

I nodded at him and struggled to free myself from a dreamlike state. My mind was stuck in the moment, the pain not allowing me to focus on anything else. The only thing I wanted was the medication that provided a temporary relief from the anguish I was experiencing.

Michael, my youngest brother, pointed at me as if directing a TV show, while Jon was the cameraman and narrator reciting to an invisible audience. "This is Anthony Aquan-Assee after eight and a half weeks, fighting, suffering and doing well. Say 'Hi' to the camera, Anthony."

"Hi" I mumbled, wondering who he was talking to.

"You look great on camera, Anthony." Jonathan said.

"Thank you," I replied, thinking how nice it felt to have my younger brother complimenting me. My mother asked if I wanted to say anything to the camera.

I had to think about it. Spontaneous requests took time for me to process. Stumbling to find the right words, I mumbled to Jonathan, "You look great up close."

Turning to my mother, I asked, "Where's my guitar?" I had always loved playing my guitar. It was a source of comfort for me and I turned to it during times of stress.

"Your guitar is at Mark's house, Anthony," interjected my father. "We have to get his permission to go into the apartment and get it," he said, sounding doubtful.

"You don't need his permission. I can give you permission," I responded, reacting like a child who doesn't get his own way. The frustration began to boil inside of me. Mark was my roommate. He and I shared an apartment before my accident. My family didn't need Mark's permission to enter my own home.

My mother was nodding her head in agreement with my father, "Anthony, you don't really need it right now. Just concentrate on getting better." She had an encouraging look on her face but the stiff posture of her shoulders and neck told me she was very worried. I didn't have the strength to argue the point with my parents.

My family sensed my agitation. I had been in this room for several days with very little stimulation. They decided to take me for a ride in my wheelchair in the main hallway outside my room. My swollen, red and blistering lips, dark, hollow eyes, and the lost look on my face worried them. They were anxious about what the future had in store for me. It was as if a stranger had taken over their son's battered body. My nurse, Joe, came in to help get me into the wheelchair so they could take me for a walk. Seeing Joe was always a comfort for me; he tended to my needs at all times.

As Joe got the chair into position I called out to my brother and said, "Help me, Mike." Mike was quickly at my side, ready to help me get into the wheelchair. My left leg was in a large red cast and I couldn't do it by myself.

"Put your arm around my shoulder," said Mike.

Groaning in anticipation of this strenuous task, I cautioned him, "Don't screw up."

My two brothers, Jonathan and Michael, were always there to help me when I needed it. Michael, with Joe's assistance, helped guide me to the wheelchair while Jonathan videotaped the entire ordeal.

Once in the chair I breathed a deep sigh of relief and moaned in pain. Any type of movement exacerbated the pain in my body. My leg with the heavy cast on it felt as if it weighed over a hundred pounds. It reminded me of the weights I used to curl with my legs when I was in training. Feeling very weak, I asked Michael to lift my leg onto the support at the bottom of the wheelchair.

Jonathan and Michael took turns pushing me down the hallway while my mother walked at my side. The change of scenery was a welcome relief. There were many other visitors standing in the hallway, however, and their stares made me feel self-conscious as I huddled beneath the blanket that kept me warm. The tracheotomy oxygen tube sticking out of my throat and the naso-gastric tube coming out of my nose made me look like an alien from outer space. The bewildered looks on the people we passed bothered me. Trying to conceal myself from their threatening stares, I hid my face with the blanket. I also commanded my brothers to take me down a deserted hallway. As they wheeled me around the hospital floor I began to get hungry, so I shouted out without regard for anyone else, "It's food time!"

Jonathan was pushing me and said in a very calming tone, "Do you want to go back to your room?"

"Yes," I replied, feeling over-stimulated by the commotion in the hallway. The brain injury left me susceptible when my senses had to take in too much information. All of the visual, auditory and tactile information that my brain had to process often led to a complete shutdown. I needed to find a quiet environment and refresh myself.

THE INTRUDERS

Late that night, the "intruders" invaded my room while I was lying in bed. I could not see them clearly in the dark. Making incomprehensible grunts they took out some rope and placed it on the bed. I started to panic. "Who are these guys and why are they here?" I thought. I was sure I was under attack.

One of the strangers grabbed my legs to restrain me and they tied my wrists to the bedside with the rope. I struggled but they were too strong. I was stuck and so afraid I couldn't speak. The ropes were secured around my wrists. I couldn't move and I had to go to the bathroom. I struggled to remove the ropes from my wrists but it was futile. Overcome by frustration, anger and embarrassment, I was forced to urinate in my pants.

The next day my father stood by my bedside, wondering why I had such a look of desperation on my face. I was demanding that he bring some knives to the hospital just in case the strange people came back to my room to tie me up again.

I pleaded with him, "Dad, bring some knives! Please!" The knives would enable me to cut the ropes that bound me. I didn't want to be alone again. I was so scared! What would happen if these strangers came back again? When could I get out of here? I wanted out of this prison!

"Anthony, you don't need any knives," replied my dad.

It turned out these strangers were the nurses and they told my father they had done it to protect me from getting up out of bed in the night and further injuring my head and my damaged knee by falling down.

I asked my father to stay with me that night. I wanted to make sure I wouldn't be alone. "That way those strangers won't come into the room and tie me up."

"Yes, I'll be staying here tonight," my father replied.

From then on, either Sherry or my father would stay with me to help keep me safe from the intruders. My father slept in the chair by my bedside and catered to all my requests.

"Dad, please stroke me," I begged him the first night he stayed; I was in so much pain. He gently massaged me. His caresses comforted me and made me feel protected. I drifted off to sleep with my father watching guard over me. He later recounted that I sat up in bed every five minutes while I was sleeping and made philosophical statements about the meaning of life. Then I lay back on the bed. I repeated this throughout the night. My father suggested that my subconscious brain was at work drawing on its acquired knowledge, making me rehearse these thoughts by speaking aloud.

THERAPY

On a very cold and snowy morning, the speech therapist came into my room. My dad was reading and keeping me company until Sherry arrived. They took turns staying with me. I was trying to stick a long thin piece of plastic down my cast to scratch my leg when a woman wearing a white coat with the sleeves rolled up to her elbows walked in. The cast was irritating me. My leg was extremely itchy but I could never reach far enough to scratch it. Feeling embarrassed, I quickly pulled out the piece of plastic and hid it under the sheets. The woman was tall with blond hair and a very warm smile. "Hello Anthony," she said. "My name is Sonya, and I'm the speech therapist. How are you today?"

I nodded my head and grumbled, "Fine."

"Good," she said. "I'm going to ask you some questions. Do you know where you are?"

I was caught off guard by the question. Why was she asking me that? "A hospital."

"Do you know which one?" she asked.

Struggling to remember what my mother had told me, I shook my head. I could not remember the name. Sonya was there to conduct a variety of language assessments and she noticed the difficulty I had communicating. The exhaustion was apparent on my face. "You look tired. You didn't sleep well last night, did you?"

"No," I said. I wished she would go away and stop asking me all these questions. The fatigue dulled my senses.

"Do you know why you're here?" she asked.

I just shook my head and responded, "No." My mind was not working! I didn't understand why she was asking me these questions. It was difficult to respond when my mind felt like it was in a cloud. When would this end?

"All these tests we'll be doing will reveal your strengths and the areas in which you're having difficulties." I sat there with a blank expression on my face, wishing my mother was there. She understood my problems more clearly than I did and she could communicate better than I could. Eventually the speech therapist left. I was tired after all the mental exercise and promptly fell asleep.

The next day was Thursday and in the morning I anxiously awaited Sherry's arrival. When someone was there with me, I felt safe. While I was watching TV, someone came into my room and startled me. I turned, thinking it was Sherry, but it wasn't. Not recognizing the person, I looked up inquisitively. The therapist said, "Good morning, Anthony. Do you remember me?"

I shook my head, wondering who she was and what she wanted with me.

"My name is Sonya. I'm the speech therapist that was with you yesterday. I'm going to show you some pictures and I want you to tell me what they are pictures of, okay?"

More work! These sessions were so draining. I knew this meant I would have to wait to see Sherry, even if she came now. The therapist would probably ask her to wait outside until she was finished. My disappointment probably showed, because she spoke to me in a soft and reassuring voice. "We'll only be a few minutes. I won't stay as long as I did yesterday." She held up some pictures and asked me to tell her what they were. She then asked me to draw pictures of certain things, and to explain the pictures to her.

These language assessments frustrated me tremendously. I could recognize what was in the pictures and knew that I had seen it before, but I couldn't find the right words to describe it. My mind could not articulate my thoughts.

I was later told that this is common in people who have sustained a traumatic brain injury. The therapist also read me a story and asked me to recall certain details. I can do this, I reassured myself, despite the fact I was unable to follow what the therapist read. I didn't remember anything she said, so I stalled for time. I made a Herculean effort to recall the story, but nothing came to me. My mind was blank. I blamed myself for not paying closer attention.

She then read me another story and when she finished it, she waited a few minutes before asking me to recall as much of the story as I could. It was very frustrating. I couldn't remember the story. I mumbled, "I can't remember the story. Can you tell it to me again?"

"I'm sorry," she said, "but I can't tell it to you again. I know this is very hard for you, but these tests are giving me a lot of information so I can help you."

The therapy sessions continued every day. There were a number of therapists who came into my room and I wasn't able to remember who they were. These therapy sessions left me feeling tired and unsociable.

HURRAY!! THE MILKSHAKE

I had been in my private room for nearly two weeks when, one cold and snowy morning, a woman wearing a white coat arrived. "We have to go for a test," she told me, "to see if you can swallow your own food. But first, I need to remove the tube from your nose. Sit up and look down while I pull the tube out."

My first thought was, What will this feel like? I did what she said and suddenly the tube was coming out of my nose. "Ouch!" was the only sound I uttered. It was a strange feeling as the tube was pulled out from deep within me. Then my nose began to bleed. "Here, put this on your nose to stop the blood," she said, handing me a Kleenex. When the nosebleed stopped, she wheeled me out of the room to go for the test.

The journey to the laboratory was very frightening. We got in the elevator and began to go down. The noise of the elevator was strange to me and it scared me. Once in the lab, another woman wearing a white coat said, "I'm going to give you a milkshake. Drink as much of it as you can." I had to drink from a straw and swallow the liquid. This was difficult for me to do and I spilled much of the milkshake when I tried to swallow. It also made me feel as if I were choking. She removed the speaking valve in my tracheotomy and said, "Now that your speaking valve has been removed, try to drink the milkshake again." They wanted to see what effect this would have on my ability to swallow the liquid. It was much harder to suck the liquid from the straw. After this experiment, a stranger wheeled me back to my room. I was exhausted and just lay on my bed and slept.

THE LAWYER DRESSED IN A BUSINESS SUIT

During the last week of November, my father, after consulting with my mother and my sister Jasmin, decided that we needed a lawyer with expertise in the area of brain injuries. I was lying in bed when my father came into my room.

"Anthony, your lawyer will be coming by for a visit in approximately one hour. His name is David Tenszen and I think you have to sign something for him." How did I get a lawyer, I wondered?

"What do I have to sign?" I asked my father.

"We have begun a lawsuit against the woman that hit you. Mr. Tenszen has agreed to take the case," he said. I trusted my father when it came to legal matters. He had taught himself law and had an understanding of what might be involved. Mr. Tenszen's firm was conveniently located near the hospital. A couple of weeks earlier, my father had visited his office and discussed my situation with him and Mr. Mandell, the senior partner. They were very helpful and informative, so much so, that my father agreed to have them represent me.

I had just finished eating lunch when David Tenszen, a tall, distinguished looking gentleman, walked into my room. Standing at the end of my bed, David looked at me with compassion in his eyes. His look told me he understood the hell I was going through.

"Hello Anthony. My name is David and I'm a lawyer with

Thomson Rogers law firm. Two weeks ago, your father came to see me to discuss what has happened to you. Anthony, with your agreement, Mr. Mandell and I will be conducting the lawsuit on your behalf. I have also brought some papers that require your signature. This is a written authorization for us to represent you." He continued speaking slowly and clearly, but it was impossible for me to focus on what he was saying. As I tried to understand his individual words, I lost the meaning of the entire message. I knew I had to sign something and since my father had agreed to have this lawyer come and see me, then it must be all right. He handed me a pen. With my signature, David Tenszen entered my life and proved to be a great support.

COFFEE WITH CREAM AND SUGAR

That night I slept badly. Since leaving the I.C.U., my sleep was restless and never refreshing, despite my being heavily sedated. I later learned that one of the areas of my brain that was damaged was the brain stem. This area controls the sleep-wake cycle. As a result, my sleep pattern was disrupted. I was continuously waking up because my damaged brain stem did not allow me to sleep for long periods of time.

My father was sitting in his chair reading his book. He looked up at me and mumbled, "Good Morning. You didn't sleep much. Are you okay?"

I shook my head and said, "No, I was scared that those guys would come in and tie me up again."

"It's okay," he replied. "I'm here with you." At that moment, one of the nurses brought my breakfast. She put the tray on the food table near me. The breakfast consisted of some scrambled eggs with toast. There was also a coffee on the tray. The coffee didn't look that great, in fact, it looked like mud and it didn't smell that appealing. I had always enjoyed fresh coffee in the morning, especially when I hadn't slept well. Looking at the coffee in front of me, I asked my father, "Dad, can you please get me a cup of coffee?" I was hoping he would get me a real coffee. I didn't want the coffee sitting in front of me. He refused. "No, Anthony, you must only drink what the doctors have decided you can drink."

"Why?" was my immediate response. "Oh, come on. I can have a coffee! What's wrong with a coffee?" I asked him.

"The doctors would not approve, Anthony!" my father replied.

I was angry that he refused to help me and I couldn't understand why. At that point I wanted to be alone and as far away from my father as possible.

The incident upset me and I felt betrayed by my father. I couldn't see that my father's refusal to get me the coffee was because he was concerned for my health. He didn't want to do anything that might jeopardize my recovery in any way. My survival, however, depended on my being focused on myself, and as a result, I had become very self-absorbed.

THE VISITS

My family came often to visit me and keep me company during the day, alternating their visits with Sherry. I began to sense that my father didn't like Sherry. She always felt very uncomfortable around him and he would be uncommunicative with her. When Sherry was in my room he would make a point of staying outside.

I was very demanding of my family and would frequently

plead, "Mom, make sure you bring my guitar." If they didn't bring it, I would be upset with them.

My friends also came to visit me often, but I felt self-conscious and embarrassed being in bed when they were there. I frequently could not remember their names. On one particular day, my friend Chris and his wife Lisa came to visit me. I was very uncomfortable as they stood at the end of my bed looking at me. In fact, Lisa excused herself to go into the hallway where she fainted. "What's wrong with Lisa?" I asked Chris.

He told me, "She's not used to seeing someone who's injured lying in a hospital bed. She just had to get some fresh air." I wondered how bad I looked. Did I look disgusting?

I didn't like being in so much pain when people were visiting me. I was also confused and unable to remember their names without thinking about it for some time. They were like strangers. Attempting to hide my confusion, I often stalled for time while I tried to remember who they were. I would ask them to get something for me and while they were busy, I would try and identify them. The memory problems haunted me throughout my recovery.

THE CHAPEL

On a cold morning at the end of November, I was lying in bed moaning and groaning, hoping that someone would come and comfort me. I turned to see Sherry sitting in the chair, worry and fear in her eyes. She looked exhausted. She had devoted so much of her time, energy, and thoughts to me and my family. She had made an extraordinary effort to balance her time between her three children, her job and me. I couldn't even acknowledge her efforts. My pain drowned any feelings of appreciation I might have had. "My leg is killing me," I mumbled. As she sat down beside me and rubbed my back, I whispered to her, "I feel so scared and tired. Help me please." Her gentle touch was soothing. She knew just how much I loved to be caressed. My father would do this to help me get to sleep. After she had been stroking me for about 15 minutes, she suddenly said, "Get up, Anthony, I need your help."

"With what?" I asked her.

"I want you to help me get you into your wheelchair."

"Why? Where are we going?" I asked, beginning to feel upset that she had disturbed me.

"I'll tell you after you get into your wheelchair."

"No! First tell me where we're going," I said, raising my voice.

"Help me get you into your wheelchair," she insisted. It was difficult for her to get me into the awkward wheelchair without assistance. She needed my co-operation. It required some maneuvering to guide me into the seat and to place my legs on the leg rests. I decided to co-operate because she had been with me all day. I raised my injured right leg onto the railing at the side of the bed, then slid my bottom over to the right side of the bed so I could sit up and turn to face the wheelchair. Sherry placed her arms around my back, giving me the support and balance I needed to guide me into the chair.

Finally in the chair, I turned to her and said, "Now tell me where!" She wouldn't tell me. She just giggled and started to push my wheelchair out of the room.

"Stop!" I shouted. "Tell me where we're going!"

"We're going on a little trip. Just sit back and relax," she said. I was getting angry and felt betrayed, but I was too weak to struggle. I just sat rigidly in the chair looking at all the people we passed on the way. They all stared at me. "I wonder what they're thinking? They must think there's something wrong with me. They must think I'm a freak."

We got to the elevator and I scowled at Sherry and didn't speak to her. Sherry placed her hand on the back of my head. "It's okay, Anthony. We're just going to the chapel. It's a beautiful place and I think you'll like it."

"I don't want to go there," I grumbled. "I might miss my medication and my leg is killing me." I was heavily dependant on painkillers and Ativan to relieve my anxiety. We took the elevator down to the third floor. I was frightened and didn't want to go to a chapel. I was not a religious person. Sherry pushed me up to a set of doors that didn't look like hospital doors. They were big, brown and majestic-looking, like the doors to a castle.

I turned to Sherry and in an angry voice said, "Take me back to my room! I don't want to be here. This doesn't look like the hospital." She told me to relax and that this was a quiet place for us to sit and rest. I was so anxious, frustrated and frightened. But once I was in the quiet chapel, it was magical and a feeling of peace came over my body. The quiet and solitude helped ease my anxiety, and I no longer craved the medication I needed to calm me.

Sherry explained that we were in the house of God and that I could pray if I wanted to. She began to pray. "Dear Lord, please help Anthony become stronger. Allow him to overcome his injuries …"

I had never really prayed before but I was awed by how peaceful I felt. I decided now was the time to start. I sat in my wheelchair beside a pew and prayed to myself. I wanted to find a way out of this hell I was living in. As I sat there in the chapel, my senses were no longer bombarded by stimuli. A warm feeling came over me and from then on I asked to be brought down to the chapel so I could find that inner peace again.

THE DOUBLE ROOM

The next day my mother told me I had to change rooms again. My insurance coverage would no longer pay for a private hospital room. I didn't want to move and protested vehemently. "Can't you do something, Mom? Call the insurance company and tell them what happened to me. They'll understand." I couldn't deal with the change. I was just getting used to the private room and knew where everything was. Going to a new room would require new learning, which was not one of my strengths at the time.

Later that day, I was transferred to another room that I had to share with a patient suffering from a tumour on his spine. I was unable to initiate a conversation with him; my problems kept me locked inside a world of my own. I had many visitors during the day to keep my mind occupied, but my confusion persisted. Everything I did required a tremendous amount of thought, especially when I had visitors. Teachers from my school would visit me and I wouldn't recognize them.

One morning an older lady came to visit me in my new room. She walked in and said, "Hello Anthony. It's nice to see you. How are you feeling?" I looked at her perplexed. I thought to myself, Do I know this woman? Who is she? Why is she here? The tension in my head was a result of the embarrassment I felt. Seeing the perplexed look on my face she said, "My name is Carolyn and I'm one of the teachers at Fern

Avenue Public School." The relief in recognizing her lasted for a brief moment but was quickly erased by an excruciating pain in my chest. I was frustrated by my inability to communicate clearly with her. My brain worked in slow motion and my cognitive problems were aggravated by the constant pain. Prior to my accident, I had always been able to grasp things quickly. Not anymore.

Carolyn spoke to me slowly and with great tenderness. I tried to focus, but the message was lost. She stayed for a while and left when a nurse came into the room.

A NEW HOME

On December 5th my mother told me I was going to be transferred to Credit Valley Hospital in Mississauga for neurorehabilitation. A new home, I thought. I would miss all the people that had become familiar to me and had helped me during some very difficult times. I had come to depend on their support and I was anxious at the prospect of leaving St. Michael's. My parents got me ready for the ambulance drive over to the new hospital. I said my goodbyes and hoped that the people at Credit Valley would be like the staff at St. Michael's Hospital.

The ambulance ride was a frightening experience for me. The sounds of traffic made me extremely anxious as I lay helplessly on the stretcher. I strained myself to look out the rear window, wondering what it would be like to be on the highway again. The ambulance attendant smiled at me. "I was one of the guys that brought you to St. Michael's way back when you had your accident. We didn't think you'd make it. It's great to see you again."

Smiling at him for a brief moment, I thanked him for his help but couldn't say more because the pain in my chest made talking almost impossible. The attendant was very friendly and pitched his voice so I could hear him over the noise of the traffic. Unable to concentrate or sustain a conversation, I closed my eyes and slept for the rest of the trip.

Once we got to Credit Valley Hospital I was taken to my new room in a wheelchair. Feeling very confused, I looked for something that was familiar – a bathroom, yes! There was one in the room and there was also the familiar metal bed. I looked around and saw several nurses but they were not the ones I was familiar with from St. Michael's. Anxiety coursed through my body. I wondered if I should ask the new nurses for some of the medication I had become so dependant on.

Some things seemed similar to the other hospital but was there a chapel? The chapel at St. Michael's had given me such peace and comfort. I hoped I could find a similar place to be by myself in this new home. Many questions went through my mind as I began to adjust to this new place. Who were all these people? Where were my mother and father? What was going to happen to me here?

A nurse wearing the familiar blue gown came into my room and introduced herself. She told me about the unit I was on and where I could get certain things. As she spoke, my mind drifted off and her words became the background to my thoughts. I needed to see someone familiar, like my family or Sherry. The nurse showed me around my room and then she asked me some questions about my family. It was difficult for me to respond to this stranger. The change of hospitals was overwhelming. I hated the idea of being a patient in yet another hospital and felt hopeless and confused about my future.

I slept restlessly that first night at Credit Valley Hospital even though I had been given a strong tranquilizer. A nurse brought my breakfast at 8 a.m. and woke me up. I looked around and didn't know where I was. The surroundings were unfamiliar and my father wasn't there. The nurse was warm and reassured me but I still couldn't remember where I was.

Finally I remembered that I had moved to a new hospital. I was relieved for the moment and inspected my breakfast carefully to see what was on the tray. Seeing what I was brought to eat became a routine that I looked forward to each morning. I was like a small child waiting for a treat.

After breakfast the nurses helped bathe and dress me. I required a great deal of direction and assistance in order to perform some very simple and basic activities. Without this assistance, I could not have dressed myself properly. I was embarrassed having someone bathe me and help me get dressed, but this was a rehabilitation hospital, my mother told me, and it was important to look my best.

For the first few days in rehab my schedule was unstructured. Initially, members of the rehabilitation team completed various assessments of me. The bewilderment of those first few days soon began to take its toll. I couldn't tolerate much activity or cognitive stimulation. The first few sessions with Colleen, the occupational therapist, took place in my room because the confusion and constant movement in the therapy room upset me.

After occupational therapy, I went for physiotherapy when the activity level in the gym was minimal. The physiotherapist agreed to see me during down times because it was easier for me to concentrate.

I was only at the new hospital for a short while when the

case manager assigned to me came and talked about the rehabilitation unit and the expectations there. Knowing the change to a new hospital was difficult for me, she spoke to my family as well. I frequently felt agitated and restless at the beginning of my stay at Credit Valley. I was confined to a wheelchair and required constant supervision because I often tried to get out of the chair. The frustration was building up inside me, but my mind kept me prisoner. I saw no solution to the problems facing me.

Being at Credit Valley was like being at school. I had to attend a variety of different therapies on a daily basis. Occupational therapy was in the morning, followed by physiotherapy. Physiotherapy was difficult because my leg still hurt a lot and I tired quickly from the exercises. It bothered me because before my accident I was in top shape. However, the dream of competing in the 2000 Olympics was far from my mind as it was very difficult to do these simple physiotherapy exercises. I did not understand why all of this was happening to me.

After physiotherapy, I often saw a neuropsychologist. The neurological/psychological assessment she conducted was frustrating. The activities challenged me tremendously. Even though I was aware of my confusion and fatigue, I was not able to see that these challenges were related to the brain injury I had sustained. Lunchtime was the highlight of my day as I looked forward to seeing what they would bring me to eat. Recreational therapy came after lunch, followed by speech therapy. Putting together proper sentences and finding the correct words to use in order to make any sense was very difficult. As a result, I frequently avoided communicating with people and tended to isolate myself.

The rehabilitation team, which consisted of the neuropsychologist, the occupational therapist, the physiotherapist, the speech therapist and some of the nurses, met regularly to discuss my rehabilitation program. Then they would meet with my family to discuss the results of their assessments and their objectives.

Being in the rehabilitation hospital was much more difficult for me than being at St. Michael's. At St. Michael's I was completely taken care of as if I were a young child. Now, in the rehabilitation hospital, I was expected to be independent and take care of many of my own needs. The staff at Credit Valley refused to listen to my constant complaining and whining. Their mission was to develop, promote and maintain my independence and daily living skills. The relearning of various activities, even something as simple as shopping, was tied into a full array of emotions.

I looked forward to frequent visits from friends to give me a break from the stresses of rehab. However, I still felt embarrassed at forgetting their names. I thought I was stupid. My friends had little understanding of my cognitive difficulties or how they might affect me, but that didn't stop them from giving me their constant support. When no one was visiting me, I would lie in my room and watch TV. My unhappiness and mental confusion sapped my energy. I felt tired, depressed, confused and lonely. I hated my life but the physical pain and mental confusion persisted for what felt like years.

THE MOOD SWINGS

Monday was the most challenging day of the week for me. The change from the weekend to the structure of regular therapy classes was a difficult adjustment. On one particular Monday, I returned to my room after an occupational therapy session in which my therapist had tried to get me to arrange some coloured puzzle pieces into a variety of different shapes. She showed me a card with a pattern on it and I had to reproduce this pattern using the puzzle pieces. It was frustrating and exhausting and I just wanted to lie down. As I wheeled my chair back to my room, I passed the nursing station and, without any warning at all, started to cry uncontrollably. I rushed back to my room as quickly as possible so no one would see me crying. Some of the visitors looked at me with concern. I was alone in the world and feeling sorry for myself. I felt trapped inside my head, which was not working as it once had. I thought, "When will this hell end? What can I do to stop this?" When I reached my room, I struggled out of my wheelchair and lay down on my bed. A nurse who had seen me crying came into my room. Trying to regain my composure, I wiped my tears and turned to face the TV.

"Are you Okay?" she asked me. "Can I get you something?"

"I'm fine, thanks. I don't need anything."

Then she said, "I know things are very difficult for you right now, Anthony. But eventually they'll get better. You might want to join the other patients in the recreation room. There's a TV there and you can play some games if you like."

I shook my head and said, "I don't want to right now. I'm tired."

"Okay. I'll let you rest and come and get you when it's time for physiotherapy."

By the time the evening came, I was exhausted, depressed and in pain. I was in my room thinking about the day's events. As I tried to organize my thoughts, I saw several other patients getting together in the hallway. They were much older than I was; at 29 I was probably the youngest patient in the rehab unit. I was very lonely. I didn't have any friends and neither Sherry nor my mother was with me.

When the nurses brought the dinner trays, the other patients drifted off to their own rooms. As I lay in bed, the tears of sadness and loneliness that rolled down my cheeks turned into deep sobs. Finally I fell asleep.

I began to experience serious mood swings that became part of my life for the next few years. On many days I only wanted to sit alone in my room and cry. The extreme swings in emotion came without any warning and I would feel either very angry or very depressed. One minute I might be feeling all right, and the next minute I would be angry and protesting vehemently. Or, I might suddenly start sobbing uncontrollably for no reason. On these days I felt helpless and out of control. The pain had robbed me of everything that was important to me, even my will to live. This emotional instability would plague me for several years.

THE PUSHUP

I had been at Credit Valley Hospital just over 3 weeks. My routine consisted of lying in bed after occupational therapy waiting for my physiotherapy class. On one particular day I began to think about the woman who had caused the accident. She had made no attempt to contact me. I had not received a phone call, a card, flowers, a note of apology, or a note asking how I was doing. I hated her. She had ruined my life. "Why me?" was all I could ask. My mood now swung towards anger, a reaction typical of the kind of brain injury I had sustained.

I wanted to go back to being the former Anthony. I didn't

want to lose the person I had been prior to my accident. I used to relish a good challenge and now I was faced with the biggest challenge of my life. As I lay there, I felt physically, emotionally, and mentally weak, but I didn't know how to get stronger. I wanted to return to the days when I was competing in both judo and bodybuilding. I struggled to the floor and positioned myself to attempt a pushup, something that had once been very easy for me. Before the accident I could do several pushups with someone lying on my back. I tried to complete a pushup but couldn't, and my efforts only increased the pain in my chest.

Rolling over I looked up at the ceiling and thought of my friend, Neil, my closest friend since grade school. Neil was a tremendous support to me when I was competing in bodybuilding. He would videotape me to show me what body parts I needed to work on for an upcoming competition. Doing pushups used to be so easy for me. Feeling depressed, I stayed on the floor of my hospital room staring at the ceiling. "What could I do back then that I can't do now?" I asked myself. I knew I felt different. I had lost so much of my brainpower, and now I knew I had lost a lot of my physical power as well. I couldn't even do one pushup.

I didn't consider the fact that just a few months ago at St. Michael's, my chest had been cut open to repair my heart. Now, after attempting a pushup, I felt as though my chest had been torn open again. I lost my motivation and got back into bed. I spent much of my time in bed and was even more despondent.

The pain caused by over-exertion stayed with me for several days. Once the pain subsided, however, I forced myself to make exercise a part of my daily routine. Just before I went to physiotherapy, I attempted some pushups and sit-ups in my room. This was my exercise time and I persevered, despite the fact that it was difficult. It required a tremendous effort to do the things that used to be easy for me. I was determined to regain my pre-accident abilities and continued to push myself towards self-improvement.

THE MOVE

In January of 1998 the hospital finalized my discharge date. After January 21 I would not need to remain as an in-patient but could continue to use the rehabilitation centre as an out-patient. After hearing the news, Sherry was as excited as a little girl. We had already decided that I would live at her house. "When you move in, things will be so great! We can finally be a family. The kids will be so happy you're there."

"They aren't the only ones who'll be happy," I replied. Worried about the tension between Sherry and my father, I whispered, "I just hope my family helps us out."

On the day I left, Sherry came to pick me up at the hospital. She supported me as I limped with a brace around my knee and used a cane. I was so happy to be leaving the hospital. As we struggled to get to her car, she insisted that I let her be my personal chauffeur. She wanted to drive me to all my appointments at the rehabilitation centre.

When we got to her house I called my mother. "Mom, it's me. I just got released and I'm at Sherry's."

"Anthony," she said, "I really wish you'd change your mind about where you're going to live. You need much more support than you can get at Sherry's house. The doctors even said that."

"Well, the doctors aren't going to determine my life for me. I want to decide what's right for me," I said angrily.

"Sherry has given me the most support. I'm sorry you can't see that!" I slammed down the phone.

I turned to Sherry. "They still think I'm a child and can't decide what's good for me! The doctors don't know everything. I hate my family!"

"Anthony, you shouldn't say that. Your family is only trying to think of what's best for you," she said. "They just don't think I'm the right person for you to be with right now, but they don't know how much I love you. Would I have stayed by your bedside almost every night when you were in the I.C.U. if I didn't love you?"

We were hugging each other when Billy, Sherry's eleven-year-old son came into the house. "Tony!!" he shouted. I'm so glad you're here. Are you staying for good?"

"Yes, I am," I told him. "I was released from the hospital today, so now I can stay here."

"Right on!" exclaimed Billy. "What's that on your leg?" he asked, looking intently at my brace.

"It's my knee brace. I tore a lot of the ligaments in my right knee. It's the ligaments that give your knee support and since mine are damaged, I need this brace."

"That sucks!" remarked Billy. He went into the TV room, flopped down on the couch and turned the TV on very loud to watch a cartoon. The noise hit me immediately. I wasn't used to hearing a TV blaring, especially when the show was a children's cartoon.

"Billy, please turn that down," I asked.

"Okay," he said.

Sherry turned to me. "You told Billy about the brace as if you were a teacher again. It was a great explanation," she said. "Come on. You must be tired. Let's go upstairs where you can lie down." She helped me upstairs and when I got to the bedroom, I started to sob uncontrollably. Sherry was already on her way downstairs to start dinner while I rested, but turned right around when she heard me crying, "Anthony, what's wrong? Are you in pain?"

"No, I'm all right," I said, struggling to regain some control. "It's just my emotions."

"Has this happened to you before?"

"Yes, many times. It happens a lot. The psychologist used some medical word to describe it at the hospital, but I can't remember what she told me."

Billy was standing at the bottom of the stairs. "What's wrong with Tony? Is he okay?" he asked Sherry. I felt bad about confusing him. Billy was a sensitive and caring young boy.

"He's fine, Billy," Sherry told him. "He's just extremely tired, so why don't you turn off the TV and go outside to play."

Sherry's two daughters, Anna and Katie, came home just before dinner, and they had the same reaction as Billy. They both ran to me and hugged me. "Tony, it's so great to see you! We missed you so much!"

"Thanks," I said. "I missed you too." The kids had come to see me in the hospital but I had not been very responsive. This was the first time they had seen me standing and looking like the Tony they knew from before the accident.

Sherry and I sat at the kitchen table eating dinner with the noise of the TV blaring in the background. Her children were laughing loudly at the program. I tried to concentrate on what Sherry was saying but the noise of the TV and the children's excited voices distracted me. Sherry saw me grimace. "Anna, Katie and Billy, please keep it down. Tony has a headache."

I blamed Sherry for my frustration at not being able to

shut out the commotion. Her children were creating confusion within me. Taking my plate, I limped out of the kitchen without even looking at her. Not wanting to make the same mistake as on the morning of my accident when I had refused to eat the egg sandwich, I carried my dinner plate with me and struggled up the stairs.

"Where are you going, honey?" She looked worried.

"Upstairs," I huffed at her. My knee was hurting terribly when I got upstairs so I put my plate on the floor and lay down on the bed. Sherry came up shortly and sat down and started stroking me. It was obvious that sitting at the table in the kitchen was not the best place for me to relax and enjoy my meal.

My sensitivity to the noises in the house continued for a long time, fuelling the emotional volatility I experienced and causing a significant amount of turmoil between Sherry and me. Frequent mood swings made me think I was going crazy. I was worried that the kids wouldn't like me as much as they used to. The constant noise from the TV room and the persistent chatter of the kids forced me to isolate myself.

What was wrong with me? These kids were going to hate me because I was always asking them to turn the TV down. But there was far too much auditory stimulation and my brain couldn't process all the information. Holding my head and retreating upstairs became a regular occurrence. The environment that I had chosen to live in after being discharged from Credit Valley Hospital was too noisy and too stimulating.

One Thursday afternoon in May, Sherry and I were sitting at the kitchen table talking about the rehabilitation hospital. I had spent the entire day in physiotherapy and occupational therapy and was extremely tired. Tears of self-pity welled up in me as we talked.

"Why don't you take off your leg brace and go upstairs and rest before the kids come home," Sherry suggested.

Mindlessly, I did as she suggested, wincing as I struggled to remove the leg brace. The pain threw me off guard and I snapped at her, "Sherry, I can't take all the noise your kids make when they come home from school. You need to control them better."

Sherry was shocked and didn't know how to respond. She finally said, "It was your choice to move in with me. You knew I had kids and that some things weren't going to change!" Her anger made me even madder. She made it sound like it was my fault.

I was aware of my own confusion and agitation but I still couldn't see that they were connected to my physical condition. Each problem that occurred was a separate incident in my mind and in no way connected to my disabilities. I attributed the impaired concentration, limited attention span, memory problems, mood swings and agitation to the challenges involved in helping raise Sherry's children. I would later realize that it was not the children that were causing me these problems. Everywhere I went the problems followed me.

After three months Sherry and I decided that I needed to be in a quieter, less stimulating environment. I decided to live with my family.

CONTINUING TO CLIMB

After Sherry dropped me off at my parents' house, I stood looking up at the window of the bedroom that used to be mine as a boy. I piled my belongings on the porch and limped into the house with the help of my cane. The impassive expression on my face hid the emotional turmoil inside me. The familiar smell of my father's curried chicken filled the house. He always cooked curried chicken when I was growing up and the smell reminded me of when I was a teenager. Pleased with myself for being able to remember something of my teenage years, I said brightly, "Hi Dad. That smells good. Can I have some?"

"Sure," he said, surprised to see me. "Help yourself. What are you doing here?"

I got myself a plate of food and sat down at the table to explain why I was home. It was unusual for my father and me to be having a meal together, just the two of us. It was also unusual for me to open up to him. Our relationship, once strained, now felt comfortable again. I thought of my father watching over me as I slept in the hospital bed.

The emotional turbulence and depression continued, however. As my sister Jasmin (a clinical psychologist) explained to the family, "The emotional injury kicks in with the partial regaining of his faculties, and this leads to depression. The depression is part of the brain injury. His dependency on heavy-duty psychotropic drugs indicates the severity of the processes he's undergoing. Anthony needs social and emotional injury rehabilitation."

On the one hand I struggled to perform ordinary mental and physical tasks, while on the other hand, my relative lack of success made me feel helpless and despondent. I was grumpy and unsociable and frequently found fault with anyone who made a noise. My brothers avoided me and eventually were scared of me, which only made me more suspicious and angry. My behaviour was making everyone uncomfortable. They all walked on eggshells trying not to disturb me.

Two days after I came home, I was in bed feeling depressed.

My brother, Jonathan, began playing a music CD he had borrowed from me some time earlier. The sound pierced my ears and I became confused when I couldn't block out the sound and focus on my own thoughts. It reminded me of the way I felt when Sherry's kids came home from school and turned the TV on loud. I thought, I can't even escape this hell in my own home. I opened my bedroom door and screamed at him to turn in off. Jonathan peered out of his room and looked at me, bewildered. This used to be my favourite CD.

Awareness of my situation only made me feel worse. I felt like a little boy trapped in a man's body. As the problems continued, so did the shouting, screaming and agitation.

I often sat at my parents' kitchen table talking to my mother, telling her my problems. My family saw things more clearly than I did. We frequently talked about how much I wanted to be a teacher again. I had loved my job and couldn't accept the doctors' opinion that I might never return to teaching. I wanted desperately to get back to the profession I so dearly loved.

On Sunday night after I had been back at my parents' house for a week, I was thinking about my future. I had just had a very lonely weekend. "Mom, what can I do? I want to be a teacher again," I said.

My mother sensed my frustration. "Well, you'll just have to relearn." Then, as if the idea had just occurred to her, she said, "You could come to my classroom and help me out if you want." She believed that volunteering would help me focus on what I was still able to do. My memory problems had blocked out a huge part of my life, including most of the things I could do before my accident.

I thought about it for a minute and replied, "Okay. What

would I have to do there?" The excitement was starting to build in me and I wracked my brain, thinking of something I could do with her students. "I know! I could bring my guitar and play for your kids."

I had not forgotten my love for my acoustic guitar. Just thinking about it gave me a tingling sensation that made me want to play again, but I hadn't practised much since being released from hospital. For a brief moment I doubted myself and didn't think I was ready to play for anyone. But in the next instant I remembered that I used to take guitar lessons in Oakville at the High Note Music Academy. I was excited because I also remembered Angelo, my guitar teacher. I decided it would really help if I started taking guitar lessons again.

"Mom, before I play for your kids, I'm going to take a lesson at High Note. I need to learn how to play again."

She was pleased. "That's great. I know the kids would love to hear you play. In fact, the other teachers in the school would love to see you too. They're always asking about you."

The next day I made an appointment for an evening guitar lesson with Angelo. My mother dropped me off in front of the music centre. My strong desire to re-learn the guitar urged me on as I struggled up to the door with my cane in one hand and the guitar in the other. Once inside I saw that the music rooms had been moved downstairs. Should I get my mother to help me, I wondered? But I knew she had probably left to go to the library and wouldn't be back until after my lesson.

As I worked to get down the stairs to the practice rooms, I noticed several people sitting in the waiting area immediately to my left. My eyes scanned the room. They looked like rock stars with their long hair, holding their guitars in their laps. They were watching me come down the stairs as though they'd never seen someone carrying a guitar in one hand and a cane in the other. Their probing looks made me self-conscious and once again I questioned my abilities. I sat in one of the chairs away from the others. I didn't want them to hear me warm up on my guitar. They were practising scales and tunes that were far more advanced than what I was capable of playing. Luckily, Angelo came and saved me from the scrutiny of these inquisitive on-lookers.

The lesson demanded a level of concentration and attentiveness that quickly drained my energy and made me feel frustrated and irritable. It looked so easy when Angelo demonstrated the songs to me with his guitar. But the coordination that was required to move my fingers in the right sequence and the ability to remember the chords seemed unachievable.

I began volunteering in my mother's classroom several days later. "Remember to bring your guitar so you can play for the kids," she reminded me. At 9:00 a.m. on Monday morning I sat in the rocking chair in my mother's classroom, holding my guitar on my lap. The school bell rang and as the students walked in, the familiar feeling of anxiety began to coarse through my body. The children looked at me curiously. The guitar instantly attracted them, like a magnet.

"Are you going to play for us?" asked a little girl crouching beside me.

"Yes, I am, but we have to wait for the national anthem first. Let's stand for *Oh Canada*." The children were breathlessly waiting for me to play. One little boy, squirming next to my mother, stood up and said to me, "Are you Superman? You look like Superman. You must be Superman." My mother grabbed his hand and said, "Chuckie, please sit down."

Another boy sitting right beside me tapped my knee brace and said, "You look like Forrest Gump with this thing on your leg."

After the national anthem, my mother introduced me. "Class, this is my son Anthony. He's the one that had the motorcycle accident. He's going to come to our class to help us when he has time. Today he's brought his guitar and will play some songs for us."

Chuckie was fidgeting with a toy car, pretending to race it. "Cool!" he said. "Do you still have a motorcycle? My dad has one. I've been on it, too."

"That's great, Chuckie." I could see he needed extra attention so I said to him, "Why don't you come here and sit beside me. I want you to pluck the strings of my guitar."

"Awwww. Can we do that too?" several of the other students asked in unison.

"Maybe later on." I replied. "Right now, I just want Chuckie to do it." This was the beginning of a relationship that I would develop with Chuckie, my mother's most challenging student. The natural skills I had as a special education teacher were coming back to me almost effortlessly. Working with kids had always been easy for me.

My volunteer work with my mother's class continued for several months. During this time I began having regular meetings with Susan, the case manager my insurance company had provided for me.

THE CASE MANAGER – THE SILENT TUTOR

In June, 1998, Susan arrived at my parents' house, promptly, for our first meeting. Susan introduced herself and told me she would be my case manager. She asked if I was okay with that. "Yes, I guess," I replied unenthusiastically, feeling drained and powerless because decisions were always being made for me. I went and sat at the dining room table feeling hopelessly inept and baffled by my situation. Life was so depressing for me. I still didn't know what I was going to do. I really didn't care who my case manager was.

Susan pointed to her notes, "Anthony, you're going to have to learn new ways of doing things. I'm here to help you with that." She was writing a note to herself on one of those yellow pieces of sticky paper.

"I use these all the time," she said. "It's a strategy to help me remember what I need to do. I don't think I could function without these stickies."

Maybe I could use those things to help me, I thought. I liked Susan's smile and her soft voice. She was dressed very professionally in trousers and a cool-coloured blouse. I was still tense but I thought, maybe she can help me. The depression was weighing me down so heavily, I felt like crying. Not wanting to cry in front of a stranger, I looked out the window and tried to suppress the flow of tears.

"Anthony, things will get better. But you need to learn new strategies to help yourself." My mother had said the same thing to me when I volunteered for her classroom. I wanted to talk to Susan about my rehabilitation, but I was too exhausted by the depression. The pain in my chest from the heart and lung surgery distracted me and drained much of my energy.

Susan looked after my case for the next two years and directed the progress of my rehabilitation activities. Her first concern was to arrange for me to begin seeing a neuropsychologist to address not only my cognitive challenges, but also the emotional problems. In the subsequent meetings we had, Susan skillfully monitored my progress and was able to arrange the necessary doctors' appointments to address my various difficulties. She also looked after all the insurance issues that would arise on a regular basis and she acted as my personal tutor, helping me cope with the challenges in my life.

BEHIND LOCKED DOORS

The emotional difficulties kept me locked up in a mind full of turmoil. At home I got more and more angry. This anger eventually turned to self-hatred and I continued to be depressed. The brain injury made me feel like a wild tiger locked in a cage. I had received a life sentence and was imprisoned inside my own head and didn't know how to escape. The need for peace and solitude became almost as strong as the need for food. Much of my time was spent just lying in bed trying to isolate myself and catch up on the sleep I never seemed to get. The most I would sleep during this time was about 2 to 3 hours a night. It affected my mental state and my ability to deal with the frustrations of daily life.

In the winter of 1999, my university friend, Sam, was talking to me outside his house. "I can't stand living at home anymore, Tony. My dad's driving me crazy."

I agreed with him. "Mine too. There are so many arguments at home. Listen," I said, "since we both hate living at home, we should get a place together."

Sam and I decided to share an apartment we found in a beautiful condominium in Mississauga. But the problems I was experiencing as a result of my brain injury continued to haunt me everywhere I turned. Like the angry tiger locked in a cage, putting another animal in the cage didn't solve the problem. I couldn't escape the hell I was experiencing and anyone too close to me felt the effects of the brain injury. There were many times when Sam could see the emotional storms raging inside me, but he couldn't unlock the doors that held me prisoner inside my mind. I was often very angry with him.

One Saturday night Sam was going out again and I was upset with him. I was jealous of his extroverted and sociable personality. It reminded me all too painfully of my social inadequacies. I still didn't like being around anyone else and preferred living a solitary existence.

I approached Sam as he was getting ready, determined to vent some of my frustration. "What are you doing?" I asked him. "Why don't you clean up after yourself? I always have to wash everything and I'm the one that cleans up in the living room. It's not fair!" I was upset at him for living the life I wanted to live.

"Tony, you know I have to work late hours. That's why I'm never home. When I get back you've already cleaned everything up so there's nothing for me to do. You're the one that's home most of the time."

He was right. My volunteer work only took up a few hours each day and much of my time was spent at home. I didn't have any other place to go. I felt like a loser because I didn't have anything going on in my life. I thought, nice friend he is. He's not the one that had a motorcycle accident. What else am I supposed to do?

We talked a bit more and he finally said, "When I come back from my date with Micky, I'll clean up in the kitchen." Sure, I thought. "Sorry, Tony," he said. "Look, here's a book I think you should read. It's by Dr. Wayne Dyer, the one who came to visit you when you were in a coma in the I.C.U."

"Thanks," I grumbled, not really interested in another

one of his apologies. But what I didn't know was that this book would be the key to unlocking my mind.

THE KEY TO UNLOCKING THE MIND

A lot of good this book will do me, I thought, if I can't even remember what I read. Before my accident, I had always loved reading. After I was released from Credit Valley Hospital I had the urge to pick up a favourite book and read it. I quickly found, however, that I was unable to read properly. Focusing my attention on the print was very hard. I didn't remember what I was reading and couldn't understand the meaningless jumble of words. After struggling with it for some time, I finally threw the book down in frustration.

I remembered that frustration as I looked at the book Sam handed me. It was his way of reaching out to me, but my physical pain, the emotional difficulties that raged in me, the sleepless nights, the memory challenges, the confusion, and the uncertainty did not allow me to see that.

"See ya later, Tony," he said as he left with his girlfriend. I was alone in the apartment again. I went into my bedroom and shut the door. The book Sam had given me was called *Manifest Your Destiny: The Nine Spiritual Principles For Getting Everything You Want*, by Dr. Wayne Dyer.

I had always loved Dr. Dyer's books and the fact that he came to visit me when I was in the I.C.U. encouraged me to continue to follow his work. I opened the book randomly at the chapter called, "You can attract to yourself what you desire: The Fourth Principle." Really? I thought. I wonder how? Intrigued, I struggled to read the first line. "The central notion of manifesting is the understanding that you have within yourself the ability to attract the objects of your desire." I re-read this line many times, trying to understand it. When it became clear to me, I felt a surge of excitement.

In searching for a key to unlock the doors to my mind, I had mistakenly thought that living with Sam would help me. To me, the solution was always somewhere outside of myself, which is why I kept moving from place to place without ever finding what I wanted. The problems had not gone away. Dr. Dyer's books and lectures taught me that the solution to any problem in life is always much closer than it appears. We all have the ability to find the solution within ourselves. "As you think, so shall you be" says Dr. Dyer.

I began thinking about how I could attract what it was that I desired. Could I find a way out of this hell? I tried to read the rest of the page but it was too difficult. It made me angry and even more determined to overcome my reading problem. From then on, every night before going to sleep I tried to read a bit of the book.

Despite the fact that I had to re-read the pages many times in order to understand what I was reading, I never gave up. Frequently, I cursed the book and threw it on the floor. Whenever I was able to read and understand it, however, I felt very good and I wanted this feeling to continue. The book was really speaking to me and I believed God was speaking to me through Dr. Dyer's words.

In the book, he says that the best way to know our future is to create it and that we can use the ability of our creative power to convert the energy of our thoughts into anything we want to bring into our lives. When I was able to under-stand this, I began to practise Dr. Dyer's manifesting medita-tions. Meditating before I went to school as a volunteer in my mother's class, and meditating after I finished my volunteer work, became a regular activity. I was able to relax and calm my nerves after being subjected to all the sensory stimulation. By meditating on a regular basis, I was ultimately able to achieve the peace and serenity I needed.

Seeing the success I was having in my mother's classroom, my case manager, Susan, organized a voluntary trial work period at Keele Street Elementary School. There I received the re-training I would need to return to work.

THE JOB COACH

Susan arranged for me to begin volunteering at Keele Street Elementary School, which is near Fern Avenue Public School. I was to have a job coach, Hugh, to help me. Feeling a surge of excitement, I asked her what I would be doing.

"You'll be working with the special education teacher there," Susan told me. "She'll show you what to do and Hugh will help you out in any way possible." Knowing there would be someone helping me was a relief and gave me a sense of security, but I was also anxious about having someone watch over me.

On Monday morning I walked into the school and went to the room where I was to meet the job coach. A man sitting on a chair stood up and said, "Are you Anthony?" I nodded and he said, "Good, my name is Hugh and I'm your job coach." He was well dressed and had an air of confidence about him.

Hugh worked closely with me and the teacher whose classroom I was in for those few weeks. But due to a sudden turn of events, he had to leave for his hometown in Nova Scotia. Changes were not easy for me to deal with so I put aside my aspirations of returning to the classroom.

My dream of being a classroom teacher was revived, however, with the arrival of a new job coach, Kim. Kim arrived at the school and came into the classroom with a cheerful smile on her face. She was warm and spoke to me reassuringly. I was eager to discuss how she could help me in the classroom, but opening up and communicating my needs to someone didn't come naturally to me. But Kim thoughtfully steered the conversation. She asked me what I needed help with the most. I learned during the next few weeks that this ability to initiate a conversation was one of her greatest strengths.

During our first few weeks together, Kim's gentle and caring manner helped me face many of the challenges in the school. When I was asked to take a small group of students to the library and go over their novel study questions with them, I turned to her and said, "How am I going to remember everything? I can't even remember what I ate for breakfast, let alone remember the names of these students." She listened to me calmly without interrupting. "You can do this, Anthony," she said.

"But there are so many things the teacher wants me to do with these kids," I protested. There's way too much for me to remember." This was my first time working with a group of students by myself. I doubted my abilities to cope but Kim showed me some strategies to help me with my memory difficulties. She helped me create a seating plan for the children in the library so I could see where each child sat and refer to the plan for their names. My confidence returned when she showed me how to break the task into smaller steps.

Kim's emotional support was a welcome relief after the struggle required just to get to school on time in the morning. The drive would leave me feeling drained and anxious before my day at school had even started. Kim also acted as a go-between with the other teachers. She helped me communicate with them and answer their teaching-related questions.

I looked forward to my interactions with Kim. She was one of the few people I dealt with on a regular basis. My desperate attempts to keep my problems hidden from the world isolated me from many people.

The memory and organizational challenges were my worst nightmare. I felt especially embarrassed and frustrated when I couldn't remember someone's name, even after they repeated it several times.

I would miss the point of what they were saying because all my energy was focused on trying to remember their name. I also found it increasingly difficult to help students with schoolwork when I couldn't remember their name.

My memory problems made it more difficult to keep my notes, lesson plans and binders organized. How could I maintain any organization in my physical world when the world inside my own head was always in a state of confusion and disorder? But these problems ceased to matter when Kim was around. She always helped me cope when I felt helpless and I was comforted because she understood.

Gradually I was given more responsibility and independence in my volunteer work. In the summer of 1999, at the end of a successful school year, I decided to fill my time by volunteering at St. Michael's Hospital. It was important to me to give something back to the hospital that had given me a second life.

I started volunteering in the neuro-trauma I.C.U. where I had been a patient for 2 months. After only one week, I saw Joe, my nurse when I was in the private room. He didn't look very happy and walked right by without recognizing me. I looked at him and said, "Joe, is that you?" He had grown a beard but he still had the strong, stocky build that set him apart from the other nurses. He slowly turned and then his face broke into a big smile.

"Anthony! What are you doing here? Are you a volunteer?" He nodded his head in appreciation when I told him that I was. Joe told me later that he was planning to quit that day until he saw me there in my volunteer jacket. He was feeling disappointed with his job and didn't think he was making a difference as a nurse. The government cutbacks to health care and the need to do more with less was taking a toll on many nurses. Seeing me there, coming back as a volunteer, made Joe realize that his work had a positive effect and that he had been able to touch someone's life – mine.

I learned many valuable lessons at St. Michael's. I realized that by extending myself for the sake of my fellow human beings, I could overcome my spiritual stagnation. By giving to and caring for others, I could give to myself. I began to grow and develop.

The doctors and the nurses found it rewarding to see a former patient who had sustained catastrophic injuries return to volunteer at the hospital.

One Saturday in July the doctors asked me to speak to a woman whose son was in a coma in the I.C.U. He had been involved in a car accident and had sustained a serious head injury. The doctors thought speaking to me might give her hope.

After our initial introductions she asked me what I remembered about being in a coma. Trying to think of the right words to say, I told her, "I don't remember anything about being in a coma but I do know that the incredible team of professionals here at St. Michael's, combined with my family's unremitting support is the reason I'm still here today. My family was always there for me, as you are for your son.

Always try to keep hope alive. This is one of the best hospitals in the world; miracles do happen here."

"I'm very happy for you," she said. "I just hope that James makes the same recovery as you. Thank you for talking with me. Your story gives me a lot of hope." I knew exactly what this woman was going through; my family had walked that very road themselves. It felt good to give something back.

THE TURNING POINT –
THE FIRST SUPPLY TEACHING JOB

In September, 1999, I returned to Keele Street Elementary School as a volunteer, but this time without a job coach. I had begun to resent having a coach, thinking it was proof of my weakness. I told my case manager at one of our regular meetings that I didn't want a job coach working with me anymore. If I was going to teach again, I would need to get used to doing it by myself. Susan listened to me without interrupting. She wasn't pleased about my decision. She knew I would be taking on a tremendous workload. "Okay," she said, "but don't you think Kim made things a lot easier for you? Do you really think you can manage without her?"

"Yes, I can do it," I replied with conviction. I must have convinced her because she started to talk about what I would need to do next. She had arranged for me to volunteer in a grade four classroom.

At first I missed Kim's support and her company. I often felt like a kitten in a lion's den. When the other teachers asked me questions, I remembered the times Kim would interject with, "Hi, my name is Kim, and I don't think we've met yet." This took the attention off me and gave me time to remember who they were. It was much harder without Kim at my side and I missed having someone to keep me company. I usually stayed by myself, trying to be invisible.

On the morning of Monday, September 13, 1999, I arrived at the school feeling tense from the emotional roller coaster I was on. Getting back to school after a weekend was always difficult for me. I walked into the grade four classroom and found the teacher at her desk, organizing some papers for the class. She looked up and smiled when she saw me. "Hi Anthony. I'm glad that you're here so early. I need some help preparing the lesson before school starts. Could you photo-copy some papers for me? I need them to be double-sided." I instantly panicked because this was something Kim used to help me with. How would I do it? Not wanting to show I had a problem, I went off to the photocopier.

The familiar feeling of dread lay heavily in the pit of my stomach. My mind struggled to find a way to begin this daunt-ing task. I needed to organize my thoughts to perform the necessary steps in the correct sequence. I felt stupid standing there beside the copier. I hoped no one would need to copy anything because I didn't want anyone to see my uncertainty. Questions began to race through my mind. Which paper should I copy first? How many should I copy? How do I make them double-sided? I was paralyzed, unable to help myself and crippled by the challenge. Photocopying is a simple task but it requires certain organizing skills essential in a teacher's life.

As I stood there trying to get control over my thoughts, the prospect of the uphill battle I faced if I wanted to return to teaching made me shudder. Teaching is a job where you depend on your memory, your organizing skills, and your ability to interact with others. I was having difficulty with all of these skills. A sinking feeling crept over me as I began to realize just how much I needed to re-learn. I wished Kim was there to help me. Eventually, I took so long the teacher had to do the photocopying herself.

At lunchtime one of the teachers asked if I was going to eat in the staff room. I immediately felt the familiar hollow feeling in my stomach again. I avoided the staff room. I became anxious talking to the other teachers, especially when I couldn't remember who they were and what they were saying. I worried about what they would say to me and what I would say to them. I usually left the school to be by myself at lunchtime. Again, my fears kept me isolated from everyone and things became increasingly difficult at the school.

As I drove home from school that day, I thought of all the strategies Kim had practised with me. I had told my case manager I could do this by myself and I wanted to do it. I knew it was essential that I continue to develop strategies to deal with my challenges.

> "Problems do not go away. They must be worked through or else they remain, forever a barrier to the growth and development of the spirit."
> ~ M. Scott Peck

One of the strategies I learned from Kim and my case manager was to write down everything I needed to remember. I became obsessive about this and it got to be very time consuming and extremely frustrating. If I didn't write something down, like a person's name, I usually forgot it. Once something was written down, however, I needed to constantly review my notes, otherwise it escaped me.

One time, I wrote down some of the things I could talk about with the other teachers. I reviewed the notes frequently just to keep them fresh in my mind. The next day I forced myself to sit in the staff room despite feeling very uncomfortable. When one of the teachers sat down beside me, I started talking to her about one of the points I had written on a piece of paper. I put the paper on the table next to my lunch so I could refer to it. My rehearsal from the night before paid off and I was able to remember most of what I had written down. The conversation went well – a pleasant change from my usual habit of sitting there with a blank expression on my face. I learned that by developing a variety of compensating strategies, I could deal with many of the difficulties associated with my brain injury.

On Friday, September 17, 1999, I stormed into my parent's house and slammed the door after a challenging day at school. My mother, who was sitting at the kitchen table reading, was startled by my abrupt entry. "What's wrong, Anthony?" she asked. She was used to seeing my angry tirades around the house, and always listened to my complaints to help me cool off.

"I can't handle working with other people. It's so difficult to achieve a common goal. Working with the kids is hard enough but when you have to team teach with a supply teacher, it's almost impossible!" I exclaimed. I'd spent my day with a supply teacher because the regular teacher had to undergo surgery and would be off for a few weeks. Adapting to someone new required a lot of flexibility, and changing my routines to accommodate someone else was not easy for me. I depended on very rigid routines. When I performed something over and over again, it became routine for me. By sticking to the routine, I learned the correct sequence of steps involved in an activity and gradually gained more control. The disruption to my routine upset me and I felt lost. But I had to work with this supply teacher, so the challenge now was to come up with strategies that we were both comfortable with. I felt myself spiralling out of control.

"Anthony," my mother said, "you're the one that had an accident. It was your choice to go to that school and volunteer. Why are you doing this if it's so upsetting to you?"

I thought carefully about what my mother said before replying. "I guess I have to put up with this until I can work by myself in my own classroom. I'll never be able to team teach again." I would never admit that my difficulties were caused by a head injury. My frustration was always the fault of the situation, the people and the events that complicated my journey back to teaching. Even driving to school made me nervous and I often called my mother for reassurance. I felt like I was losing my mind and just wanted to end this agony, but I persisted because I didn't want to admit defeat.

One day the vice-principal approached me and said, "Anthony, we're in a jam. Bev's away and we don't have someone to cover her grade 2 class. Since you have your teaching qualifications, would you be able to cover her class this afternoon?" I felt a surge of anxiety knowing I would have to do it by myself. But my anxiety quickly turned to excitement when I realized I would be teaching by myself for the very first time.

"Yes! I can do it," I said. "No problem."

I immediately went to the library to find as many books as I could to read to the kids. I also planned some extra activities just in case they ran out of things to do. Sitting in the library at lunch, I was as nervous as a student teacher going into their first classroom. But the nervousness was mixed with an excitement I had not felt before. I hadn't been in a classroom alone with students since before my accident. Could I do it?

The bell rang and startled me back to reality. Picking up my things, I walked briskly to the grade 2 classroom, demonstrating a confidence I didn't feel. Many of the grade 2 students were wandering around the hall, some looking for the water fountain, others looking to see who their afternoon teacher would be.

"Hello," I said. "My name is Mr. Aquan-Assee and I'll be your teacher this afternoon. Let's go inside."

Once inside the classroom, we sat down in a circle and I began the afternoon by reading a story I had chosen from the library. As I began to read, I remembered that only a few months ago it had been a struggle for me to read a book. After finishing the story, the kids were very quiet and the enthusiastic look on their faces told me they wanted me to continue reading.

When I put the book down, a boy sitting close to me raised his hand and asked, "Why do you have a hole in your neck?" He was pointing at my tracheotomy scar.

"Well, I had to have an operation in the hospital," I told him. The class then spoke in unison, "Cool, wow." These kids were so observant and curious, I wondered if they noticed the scar from my heart surgery that extended to my tracheotomy scar.

The rest of the day went smoothly and I was able to introduce some of the activities I had planned. I began to feel competent and confident in my ability to manage a class. At the end of the day, several students came up to hug me before going home. "Goodbye Miffter A." Holding back the tears and struggling to control my quivering voice, I hugged them and said, "Goodbye. Thanks for a great afternoon." I was so happy I wanted to cry. Some of the parents arriving to pick up their children smiled as they watched their child say goodbye to me. The nervousness I felt at the beginning of the afternoon turned into gratification as the kids left the classroom. I had completed a very successful supply-teaching job. I had been able to do the work by myself without any support.

As I drove home, a feeling of joy came over me. Sobs shook my body as I was overcome with emotion. I knew I had accomplished so much just to get to this point and I knew I could do it again. When I got home, I found my mother in the kitchen preparing supper.

"Mom! You'll never guess what happened today! I taught a grade 2 class by myself and the kids loved me!" Hearing my exciting news, she smiled. She had been praying for a change and it seemed as if her prayers had been answered.

"Why don't you call your case manager and tell her the news? This is fantastic. I'm so happy for you." I called Susan and told her.

"Wow! What great news, Anthony. I couldn't have planned it any better myself. Maybe they'll ask you to do it again. What a great way for you to get back into teaching." I could hear the happiness in Susan's voice and knew this was the start of big things to come.

In October, 1999, I called the new principal, Faegi, at Fern Avenue Public School, my former school. She sounded surprised but glad to hear from me.

"I've heard so many good things about you, Anthony. We'll have to meet sometime soon. I have some news that might interest you. Judy, the special education teacher is retiring in December. You remember her don't you?" I was caught off guard and couldn't remember who Judy was so I lied, "Yes, I know her."

"We'll be needing another special education teacher and since your name is still on our staff list, I was wondering if you'd be interested in the position?" I couldn't believe what Faegi had just asked me.

"Yes, I'm interested!" I answered enthusiastically. A teaching job! I was ecstatic. But my heart sank when I remembered I needed medical clearance before I could return to work. The next day I spoke to my neuro-psychologist who said, "I can tell you're doing much better, Anthony, but I'm not a teacher so I can't say whether you're ready to return to teaching yet. I need to get some evaluations from the other teachers as well as from the principal. As soon as I get these evaluations I can write a letter to the Toronto District School Board clearing you to return to work."

Anxiety gripped me. I had to prove myself to the other teachers before I could work again. "Okay, Dr. B. I'll do it," I whispered. I trembled as I thought of how much effort would be required.

The next day at Keele Street Public School, I approached the principal, Jon, and asked him, "Would you be able to evaluate me during a teaching situation and then write a letter confirming your evaluation to my neuro-psychologist?"

"Sure," he said. "We can do it this afternoon."

"Thanks" I replied, nervously. I hadn't expected it to be so soon. During lunch I was very quiet, knowing I was going to be evaluated by the principal. My throat was constricting with anxiety and I could barely swallow my food.

That afternoon I was teaching the grade 2 class in the gym. Dread swept over me when Jon come in and nodded at me to begin the lesson. He watched me carefully as I explained the gym activity to the children. But he smiled when he saw the children participating with so much enthusiasm in the activities I had planned. The smile on his face and the laughter of the children made me tense up because I was afraid I might start crying. I could feel that things were going well, though, and it made me feel good. This kind of emotional situation often resulted in the drastic mood swings that brought me to tears. Luckily, I was able to maintain my composure until the end of the lesson.

Jon came up to me. "Great work, Anthony. I'll type up this evaluation and give it to you in a day or two, okay?" Feeling a tremendous sense of relief and satisfaction, I could only nod and say, "Thanks a lot."

I took the students back to their homeroom and sprinted to the staff washroom where I could cry in privacy. I had no control over the tears. My emotions raged inside of me regardless of where I was. But my tears did not diminish my feeling of triumph. I'd successfully taught a physical education lesson to the grade 2 class and I'd remembered everything I had to say. I eventually stopped crying and I thrust my arms exuberantly into the air, relishing my victory.

Several days later the Keele Street vice-principal had to evaluate me. She observed me teach a lesson to the special education class. I had reviewed what I would say and what I needed to emphasize many times and the lesson went very well. In order to remember something, I reviewed it obsessively. The obsessive tendencies that a psychiatrist had noted following my accident were now helping me cope with my memory problems.

Various classroom teachers also evaluated me as I taught lessons with different classes. I gave their letters of evaluation to my neuro-psychologist. Dr. B. read them and nodded his head in approval. "It looks like you've impressed the staff at Keele Street, Anthony. They all support your return to teaching, so I'll be able to write your return to work letter. You've worked extremely hard, Anthony. You deserve this."

My case manager and I decided I should volunteer at Fern Avenue Public School in the special education class I was hoping to take over. It would be a good transition for me since I would eventually be taking over as the teacher in this classroom.

My vision of returning to teaching was starting to become a reality, but the price of my success made me wonder just how long I could keep up the effort. The move to Fern Avenue meant I had to say goodbye to the staff at Keele Street and goodbye to the safety net of being a volunteer. At Fern Avenue, I would be a teacher who had to know what to say and do without rehearsing obsessively ahead of time.

Saying goodbye to the staff at Keele Street was difficult but I knew my continued rehabilitation depended on it. The move towards more independence is a necessary part of the journey through rehabilitation. With much apprehension, I said my goodbyes to the staff at Keele Street Public School, and prepared to face my fears at Fern Avenue.

I experienced a lot of frustration, sadness, and anxiety adjusting to Fern Avenue. The effects of my traumatic brain injury were invisible; the rest of the world couldn't see them. But having a brain injury didn't mean I couldn't function at a high level. It just meant that I had to re-learn many things, including various teaching strategies and practices, and effective classroom routines. I also had to acquire new life strategies for coping with daily challenges and issues. Developing and mastering these compensating strategies enabled me to move forward in my journey out of brain trauma. With much assistance and encouragement from others, I have been fortunate to escape many of the handicaps of a brain injury.

On January 3, 2000, I stood in front of my class of students, excited at the prospect of a new year. I had arrived at school at 7:00 a.m., anxious to begin the first day of the rest of my life. "Good Morning, boys and girls. It's great to be starting this new year as your teacher. This will be a very special year for all of us. We will all see many changes within ourselves. Let's help each other to learn and to grow." Little did my students realize just how much I had to re-learn. With those words I closed many doors to my past, but I opened up many new doors to my future.

I continued to push myself forward on my climb up the ladder of life. It required the tremendous help and support of the many people with whom I came into contact. These were the outstanding professionals that worked with me in and out of the hospital setting, and the many friends that supported me and my family. But, most importantly, my family was the spark that lit the flame inside me so I could continue to climb. Despite all the difficulties I still face, the accident helped me discover myself, my work, my mission and my God.

God Bless you all and thank you for sharing my story.
Anthony Aquan-Assee

The things which hurt, instruct.
~ Benjamin Franklin

Anthony and Dr. Andrew Baker, Director of the Neuro-Trauma
I.C.U. at St. Michael's Hospital. He was one of the doctors
involved in my care in the I.C.U.

Second Life, Second Chance!

Tools for Empowerment

Healing comes only from that which leads the patient beyond himself.

~ C. G. Jung

Jung's words in mind, I knew that I could heal myself with the right thought, the right action, prayer and meditation. I have devoted my entire life to a quest for the tools to heal myself. Following are the tools and strategies I used to assist me to ride the waves of this storm and continue to climb the ladder in my life.

Many people have a wrong idea of what constitutes true happiness. It is not attained through self-gratification, but through fidelity to a worthy purpose.
~ Helen Keller 1880 – 1968

GOAL SETTING

During my recovery, I knew I had to take charge of my life. Proactive people work on the things they can do something about while accepting those things they can't control. They take the initiative and responsibility to make things happen. Waiting around and continuing to feel sorry for myself would not bring me what I wanted. After Sam gave me the book, *Manifest Your Destiny: The Nine Spiritual Principals of Getting Everything You Want* by Dr. Wayne Dyer, I began to picture myself teaching in a classroom filled with students. These mental pictures allowed me to keep my thoughts focused on my ultimate goal, which was to return to teaching. As Dr. Dyer put it, I was visualizing in great detail what I wanted to manifest or bring into my life. Identifying my goals gave me a perspective on my life and it also gave me a sense of direction.

Setting goals allows us to choose the direction we want to go in life. It gives us a long-term vision of our future and helps us concentrate on reaching this vision.

The medical professionals doubted that I could return to teaching. But by setting specific, measurable and realistic goals,

I was able to achieve my goal. An effective goal identifies not only where we want to be, but also where we are in the present so we can see where we are in relation to that goal. By writing our goals down, we become like the captain of a cruise ship consulting a map prior to departure. We remind ourselves of our intended destination. We can then plan our daily activities, be proactive and take charge of our life.

Focusing on my goals allowed me to concentrate during times of uncertainty. My goal to return to teaching gave me certainty during the uncertain time of my rehabilitation. Although I was hampered by many disruptions and aggravations, I always kept my goal of returning to teaching at the front of my mind. Awareness of my desired destination enabled me to gear all my efforts and energy towards reaching that destination. Without a goal it would have been easy to let my frustrations take over and eventually I would have given up. My intention of returning to teaching guided me in making the right decisions and taking the actions necessary to make it a reality.

I encountered many roadblocks along the way. One of my goals was to strengthen my body, particularly my leg, with regular daily exercise at the gym. I could not always get motivated to face the struggles I experienced at the gym. Many times I would resort to old habits and just lie on the couch and watch TV. When this happened, I had to re-focus on my goal and remind myself of the SMART principal for setting goals: Goals must be **S**pecific, **M**easurable, **A**ttainable, **R**ealistic, and the **T**ime to attain them must be stated. Sometimes re-focusing during these periods of apathy enabled me to break down the larger goal into smaller, more manageable mini-goals. Instead of completing my entire workout, I focused on one exercise. This allowed me to feel I had accomplished something in line with my ultimate goal.

It's important to have some structure in place to help us stay motivated. My "To Do" checklist helped keep me on track to complete the activities that supported my rehabilitation and my volunteer work. Everything I had to do each day was written down on a checklist the night before. In the morning, I would look at my "To Do" list and see what I needed to accomplish. The items on my list were prioritized in order of importance. If I had to go to the gym and exercise my aching leg, I wrote it on my checklist. If I had to talk to someone at my volunteer workplace, I wrote it down. Even though I usually avoided speaking to people, if it was on my "To Do" checklist, I made an attempt to do it.

Checking off the completed activities motivated me to finish the other activities on the list. It required self-discipline to continue with this each day. At the end of the day, however, it was very rewarding to see all the items checked off. It meant I had a productive day. I'd make another list to prepare me to face the next day and ensure it was also a productive day.

Focusing on my goals helped expand my universe. The future belongs to those who believe in the beauty of their dreams.

Controlling Our Thoughts and Our Emotions

Men are disturbed not by things, but by the view which they take of them.

~ Epictetus 50 — 120

COGNITIVE THERAPY

The second tool I successfully used in my recovery was controlling my attitude by controlling my thoughts.

Life deals us a variety of situations that we react to with a variety of emotions: happiness, anger, sadness, anxiety and fear. Our attitude, which is under our control, determines our reaction to events. Our attitude determines how we see a situation and how we feel in that situation. How we think determines how we feel. To change our attitude, we must either change the way we think or the way we act.

The idea that our thoughts influence our emotions and behaviour is the basis of cognitive therapy. Cognitive therapy is an educational therapy where a person learns how to change the way they think in order to change the way they feel. Thought usually precedes emotion and determines feelings, so a certain thought will result in a certain feeling. Cognitive therapy consists of learning how to connect your emotions to your thoughts. Most of the time our thoughts go by very quickly, but we can learn to focus on them and take note of them.

It's not what happens to you, but how you react to it that matters.
~ Epictetus 50 - 120

With the help of my neuropsychologist and my support group, I was able to change much of my thinking, which helped me change my feelings and my attitude.

For example, when I was volunteering at Keele Street Public School, I avoided the staff room at lunch because I was self-conscious and didn't want anyone to think there was something wrong with me. My thoughts were filled with images of the teachers thinking negative or critical things about me and that, because I had these challenges, there was something wrong with my character. These insecurities paralyzed me and prevented me from acting on my fears.

My neuropsychologist suggested I try thinking the other staff members were happy that I was joining them in the staff room and didn't notice the difficulties I was experiencing. By changing my thinking, I changed the way I felt and was able to enjoy my lunch in the staff room with the other teachers. My neuropsychologist also helped me focus my thoughts on all the things I had overcome instead of the obstacles in my life.

People respond to stressful situations based upon their past learning experiences, often resulting in exaggerated emotional reactions. The thoughts that come before emotion may not be logical, and are usually based on beliefs that are acquired early in life from parents, relatives, friends, teachers, and/or religious training. However, these beliefs were acquired through the eyes of a child. The actual communication may have been distorted, observed in the magical world of childhood, and accepted without question. But they form the basis of how we perceive situations that present themselves in our adult lives.

The problem begins when our immediate thoughts are not rational or logical and the resulting emotions are negative or hurtful. The goal of cognitive therapy is to correct errors in thought and help modify the beliefs that serve to maintain these maladaptive emotions. Through careful analysis and introspection, irrational thoughts and beliefs can be transformed into a realistic appraisal of a situation, leading to a change in feelings.

When someone feels bad, it's because they see their situation from a negative perspective. Their negative evaluation of the situation leads to negative thoughts. And their negative thoughts make them feel bad. Dr. Albert Ellis refers to this pattern as the "A-B-C" of emotion.

> **"A"** stands for the "actual event" that led to the
> emotion.

"**B**" stands for one's "beliefs" about the event,
the thoughts that take place after the event.
"**C**" stands for the "consequences" of one's beliefs
or thoughts, the way one feels or behaves.

An example that illustrates this pattern occurred when I was volunteering at Keele Street. I always experienced feelings of anxiety when I was speaking to a person whose name I had forgotten. This happened many times with the same individual during the course of a day. As a result, I frequently had to ask them to repeat their name. It made me think there was something wrong with me and I felt worthless, self-conscious and stupid.

When we are aware of our negative thoughts, or cognitive distortions, we can see the error in our thinking. The thoughts can then be changed, resulting in a change in feelings. With the help of my neuropsychologist I learned to focus on my positive qualities to combat my negative thoughts.

It's important to keep in mind the words of Dr. Dyer: "As you think, so shall you be." The web of a negative thought will capture other negative thoughts lurking nearby and ultimately corrupt the spirit. By working through the difficult periods in our lives and identifying the errors in our thoughts, we become whole and healthy, build self-confidence, awaken and express new and more powerful aspects of ourselves.

Life's challenges are not supposed to paralyze you;
they're supposed to help you discover who you are.
~ Bernice Johnson Reagon

CHALLENGE YOUR THINKING

Once the cognitive distortion that is associated with automatic thought has been identified, it is then possible to correct the errors in thinking. The following steps are used in cognitive therapy to deal with errors in thinking:

1) Identify the problem by writing a description of the upsetting event on paper, in very specific terms.
2) Record the negative feelings that are experienced as a result of the situation.
3) Try to identify the automatic thoughts that are associated with the negative emotions. What exactly are the messages the person is telling himself or herself? They are called automatic thoughts because when someone feels upset, these thoughts come to mind automatically, without any effort.
4) Identify the cognitive distortions associated with each automatic negative thought. For example, someone might be looking at a situation from an all-or-nothing perspective. They might also be jumping to conclusions or blowing things out of proportion. These are examples of distorted negative thoughts.

5) Examine the evidence for the automatic thought. Once the facts are carefully examined, it's possible to see things from a different perspective. Substitute more rational and realistic thoughts in place of the negative automatic thoughts.

We frequently blame external forces for our feelings and our attitudes. By looking outside ourselves for the problem, we lose the power to control our attitude. When we look inside ourselves for the problem, we control the outcome and we empower ourselves to deal with the problem effectively. We are always responsible for our attitude regardless of the situation we find ourselves in. A person can have either a positive or negative attitude, but, with the right attitude, that person can be strong and face those ups and downs we all experience.

To begin changing their own feelings, a person might want someone else to change their behaviour. However, they're making the mistake of looking outside themselves for the solution to their problem, thus losing control of the solution. We must control ourselves before we can control someone else. In addition, someone might depend on alcohol and/or drugs to feel better. These external substances might help them feel better temporarily, but they are just escaping from their real feelings. As a result, they lose power over the solution. The solution to every problem lies inside us.

The next time you feel "bad," don't ask yourself, "Who did this to me?" but rather, "What have I been thinking? What have I been telling myself?" By turning inward, you may find that it was your inner dialogue that caused the emotional distress.

To control our feelings, the first thing we must do is identify the negative thoughts that have contributed to our negative state of mind. Every negative feeling results from a specific kind of negative thought. Sadness and depression, for example, result from thoughts of loss.

It's important to stop the cycle of negative emotions, by identifying and stopping negative and unconscious "self-talk." This negative talk is automatic and we have programmed our internal computers to react and think in a self-defeating way. Only by stopping these automatic negative thoughts can we experience our own power and joy.

_____

As You think, so shall you be.
~ Dr. Wayne Dyer

_____

Face Your Fears

Each problem is an opportunity in disguise.
~ Dr. Wayne Dyer

It is possible to view the problems and obstacles in our lives as precious gifts. Our lives change when we become conscious that every difficult and frightening experience has a purpose. There is a reason for everything that happens to us. We can run from our problems, but we can never hide from them. Feeling fear is not a good reason to avoid something in your life. Your fears will always follow you wherever you go. By facing our fears, we learn ways to deal with them so that we no longer live in fear.

Fear was the predominant feeling during every stage of my recovery. I got tired of running from my fears and finally realized I needed to face them and stop running from them.

When I was volunteering at Keele Street, my fear was intense and I avoided the staff room because of it. Fear determined my behaviour every day. To deal with it, I decided to write down a variety of things to say in certain situations and I rehearsed them frequently so they became automatic. Then I forced myself to go into the staff room and talk to a teacher about some of the things I had rehearsed. I soon realized that the other staff members did not see me in a negative way and I felt relieved. With energy and effort you can identify exactly where your stress is coming from and take the necessary steps to minimize it.

Obstacles don't have to be the end. Instead, they can provide the motivation to change your life. The first step in this process of change is to put your priorities in order, to know what it is you most desire. Then outline the necessary steps to reach your objective and direct your efforts towards these steps.

One of the secrets of life is to make stepping stones out of stumbling blocks.
~ Jack Penn

Focusing on priorities and controlling our thoughts requires that we quiet the inner dialogue in our mind. The tools I used to accomplish this were deep relaxation and meditation. Deep relaxation and mediation helped me take charge of my life instead of depending on medication to ease my anxiety.

Meditation is a technique, or a practice, that calms the mind and pushes away the incessant chatter of our ego. It usually involves focusing attention or concentration on an object, such as a flower, a candle, a sound or word, or on our own breathing. It is a state of being in the moment, an experience of silence, without thought. Meditation enables us to quiet the mind, allowing it to become peaceful, calm and focused. It also frees us from the barrage of sensory stimulation in the world.

Western medical authorities now recognize the benefits of meditation. Meditation can be practised as a basic relaxation technique using these simple steps:

1. Sit or lie in a relaxed posture. You should feel comfortable without moving.
2. Keep your back, neck and head aligned. Relax your shoulders and find a comfortable place for your hands.
3. Focus your attention on your breathing. Pay attention to your breath as it flows in and out. Whenever you find that your attention has moved elsewhere, just note it and gently bring your attention back to your breathing. By chanting a "mantra" you can free yourself from the thoughts that occupy the mind. The word mantra comes from the Sanskrit *man* (mind) and *tra* (sound). It involves focusing on a thought through the repetition of sounds, words or phrases. This type of meditation allows you to forget the body and experience a state of relaxation. It's important to find a method of meditation that works best for you and to practice it regularly.

Some people achieve a meditative state through such things as exercise, running, dancing or Tai Chi. Other people can achieve a state of meditation through an activity or event that brings joy or beauty, such as a sunset, a beautiful flower, the swaying of the trees, the roar of the ocean, or a loved child or pet.

There are many benefits to meditation as a regular practice. Along with the spiritual benefits are increased relaxation, increased mental focus, peace, reduced stress, lower blood pressure, and lower pulse. Integrating relaxation and meditation into my daily routine has greatly improved my health and my spirituality. It has transformed my life by allowing me to focus on what I really want in my life.

On September 23, 1997, I was knocked off the ladder of life. Before my accident, my search for happiness revolved around my pursuit of external sources of comfort. I say external because I never looked inside myself for happiness. I was happy only when other people acknowledged my good qualities. The low points in my life led me to doubt the presence of a God or any other supernatural being or force. I did not see the connection between the events in my life.

Looking back, it seems as if my personal experiences were carefully planned to prepare me for what lay ahead. It was as if I had an invisible team of strategic planners working on my behalf, without my knowledge, to ensure the correct sequence of my life's events. Most importantly, the events leading up to the day of my accident enabled me to deal with the cognitive, emotional, physical and social changes brought about by the accident.

The rewards of my brain injury have been priceless. In order to cope with the problems associated with my brain injury, I had to re-learn so much. In essence, it was a re-birth made possible by the help of many people who entered my life. Some of these people played only minor roles in my recovery, while others played starring roles for a longer period of time.

More than anyone, my family helped produce and direct the show called "Anthony's Life." Through their love a spiritual awakening was born in me, out of the ashes of despair.

I have learned that love is the subtlest force in the world. All of the problems in my life were made easier because I was loved. I have now reached a place where I can look back at all the people in my life and realize that they all had something to teach me. With these lessons I have been able to face my traumatic brain injury.

In this world you will encounter many problems and challenges, with many lessons to be learned. To realize your full potential, surround yourself with the love of those who encourage you to be all that you can be. Recovering your capacity to function more effectively after a brain injury requires the support and love of those close to you. It is through our interactions with others that we discover ourselves.

He who conquers himself is the mightiest warrior.
~ Confucius 551 — 479 B.C.

References

Beck, A.T. "Thinking and depression: 2, Theory and therapy." Archives of *General Psychiatry*, 1964, 10, 561-571.

Beck, A.T. *Cognitive Therapy and Emotional Disorders*. New York: International Universities Press, 1976.

Burns, D.D. *The Feeling Good Handbook*. New York: The Penguin Group, 1989.

Covey, Stephen. *The 7 Habits of Highly Effective People*. New York: Simon and Schuster Inc., 1989.

"Choosing With Pride": A Career Education Curriculum Resource for Grades 7 & 8: Toronto District School Board.